Retiring

Without

Risk:

"Finding Shelter From Financial Storms"

Other Books By:

Roccy DeFrancesco, JD, CWPP, CAPP, MMB

The Home Equity Acceleration Plan (H.E.A.P.™)

www.heaplan.com

The Doctor's Wealth Preservation Guide

www.physiciansfortress.com

The Home Equity Management Guidebook: How to Achieve Maximum Wealth with Maximum Security

Wealth Preservation Planning: A "Team" Approach

Retiring Without Risk:

"Finding Shelter From Financial Storms"

By:
Roccy DeFrancesco, JD, CWPP™, CAPP™, MMB™
Founder: The Wealth Preservation Institute
Co-Founder: The Asset Protection Society

This publication is designed to provide accurate and authoritative information regarding the subject matter covered. It is presented with the understanding that neither the publisher nor the author is engaged in rendering legal, accounting, or other professional services through the issuance of this book. If you need individual advice on the topics covered in this book, please contact the author or another qualified professional for an individual consultation. Also, always seek counsel from an advisor before taking actions based on this or any book. Laws and products change rapidly, and you want to make sure when you implement a plan that it is based on the most up-to-date information possible.

The Retiring Without Risk™ book cover was designed by **Patrick Yore** of Brainblaze, LLC (http://www.brainblaze.com).

Retiring Without Risk™

By: Roccy DeFrancesco, JD, CWPP™, CAPP™, MMB™

Copyright © 2009 by TriArc Advisors, LLC

TriArc Advisors, LLC
3260 S. Lakeshore Dr.
St. Joseph, MI 49085
269-216-9978
313-887-0532 (fax)

ISBN-13: 978-0-9770770-8-3

This book is dedicated to all readers
who would like to build wealth while not having to worry about
what happens when the stock market crashes like it did from
2000-2002 (-46%) and again in the early part of
2007 to the early part of 2009 (-59%).

.

I hope you enjoy reading this book as much as I enjoyed writing it.

Roccy DeFrancesco, JD, CWPP™, CAPP™, MMB™

MONEY EQUITY MANAGEMENT
GUIDE BOOK
PAGE # 54

Table of Contents

Retiring Without Risk

FINDING SHELTER FROM FINANCIAL STORMS

<u>Acknowledgements</u>

With any book that covers n financial planning/wealth building concepts, it is rare for an author to not have help/input from multiple people or sources. This book is no different.

Always at the top of my list are my two loving children Lauren and Mitchell. They are my inspiration.

On the technical side of the book, I have several people to thank as this book covers several different subject matters (traditional wealth building, cash value life insurance, annuities, fixed indexed annuities, guaranteed return/income product, financial planning, etc.)

In alphabetical order, I'd like to thank the following people for their contributions to this book:

Todd Batson, Lawrence Bedard, Charlotte Bewersdorff, Bill Curry, Carl Curry, Marcia DeFrancesco, Roccy DeFrancesco, Sr., Mike Duncan, Timothy Frisby, David Gimple, Jayne La Blanc, Steve Locko, Ted Leutz, Richard Migliaccio, William Newport, Lynette Robbins (of the Knowles System), Jason Ruggerio, Greg White, and Patrick Yore.

Preface

My guess is that virtually everyone reading this book has seen one or more infomercials on how to "get rich quick" or get rich with "no risks" and "no worries."

Have you ever read an ad to attend a seminar that, if attended or bought a book that, if read, would teach you the "secrets" wealthy people use to become wealthy. I'm sure the answer for many readers is yes.

For some reason, people believe that wealthy or affluent people in our country have access to or knowledge of "secret" wealth-building tools that the "average" American is not privy to.

Over the last ten plus years as an educator of advisors, I've seen a lot "magic pill" wealth-building plans come and go. As the founder of <u>The Wealth Preservation Institute</u>, it my job to research, form an opinion, and educate advisors on old and new wealth-building and asset-protection tools.

What I can tell you for a fact is that there is <u>NO SUCH THING</u> as a "secret" wealth-building tool. There is <u>NO SUCH THING</u> as a "magic pill" you can take that will help you build wealth with no risk, no worries, and guaranteed success.

As a general statement, in order to grow wealth, you need money. That might sound like an obvious statement, but there is no wealth-building tool in the world that does not revolve around using money to grow more wealth.

Do you know how most people became wealthy? I'm sure you already know the answer. Besides inheriting it, most worked hard and had good support from family, friends, and colleagues to help them along the way. Dare I say that some wealthy people also may have had a little luck on their journey to become wealthy? Sure. It never hurts to have a little luck in anything you do (like getting out of the stock market before the crash of 2000-2002 and again in 2007-2009).

While I'd like to tell you that I have some "secret" plan to help you build your wealth in ways that no one else knows, that is not the case. No such plan exists (no matter what a local advisor, talking head on radio or television, or author has been telling you).

Having said that, what you will read in this book will be new to most readers and will give you insight into alternative ways to "Retire Without Risk."

As we've all found out, the <u>stock market really doesn't grow at 12% a year</u>. In fact, sometimes it goes <u>backwards 59%</u> over a several-month period (like it did at the end of 2007 through the beginning of 2009).

The tools discussed in this book are widely known by many financial planners, CPAs, and life insurance advisors. However, while most advisors know about these tools, the vast majority <u>do not understand their power and protective features</u> which make them ideal wealth-building tools for many Americans.

My goal with this book is very simple. I want you to understand the tools discussed to such a degree that you will understand specifically how they and also have a good idea if one or more of the tools may be useful in a plan to help you "Retire Without Risk."

If read this book and find anything unclear, are having problems understanding the value of the various tools, or if you wonder specifically how to use one or more of the tools in your wealth-building plan, please feel free to contact me with questions. I am going to give you my personal e-mail address (<u>roccy@retiringwithoutrisk.com</u>) and my direct office phone number (269-216-9978).

Please do not hesitate to contact me. I would be more than happy to answer your questions and then refer you to a qualified advisor who can help you in your local area.

<u>Foreword</u>

This book is dedicated to readers who are looking for understandable answers to the following questions:

1) Is investing money in the stock market the "best" place to grow wealth?

2) Notwithstanding all the hype about how well the stock market has done over the last 20+ years, what are the real statistics showing what the "average" investor has actually earned when invested in the stock market (the answer is shocking)?

3) How do you build a tax-free retirement nest egg in the most efficient and **<u>least risky</u>** manner possible?

4) Does it make financial sense to overfund a tax-deferred qualified retirement plan or IRA?

5) Is "Revolutionary Life" insurance a good financial tool to build wealth for retirement?

6) Are there wealth-building tools that can **<u>guarantee you a 7%+ rate of return</u>**?

7) Are there wealth-building tools that can **<u>guarantee you a lifetime income</u>** you can never outlive?

If you find the above questions interesting, you will certainly enjoy this book.

WHY YOUR ADVISORS WILL NOT KNOW MANY OF THE TOPICS COVERED IN THIS BOOK (OR IF THEY KNOW THE TOPICS, WHY THEY LEARNED THEM FROM BIASED SOURCES)

Why advisors do not know many of the topics covered in this book is a very common question I receive when educating clients on the concepts covered.

The main reason local advisors do not know many of the topics covered in this book is because there is no formal educational body in the country that educates on them.

Let me restate that; I cover the topics discussed in this book in much more detail in the <u>Certified Wealth Preservation Planner</u> (CWPP™) course (<u>www.thewpi.org</u>) that is offered through The Wealth Preservation Institute. However, the course is very intensive and geared towards advisors who have or want to have an affluent client base. Therefore, I only have 75-200 advisors take my courses per year. My point being that 99% of the advisors out there (CPAs, attorneys, financial planners, insurance advisors) do not know much of what you'll read about in this book.

BIASED SOURCES

One of the reasons I decided to write this book is because I have grown tired of the hypocrisy I've seen over the past many years in the financial services industry (which has gotten worse over the last few years).

What hypocrisy?

What I'm about to tell you is not known to 99.99% of the consumers (non-advisors) in this country.

<u>Broker Dealers</u> (BDs)—Do you know what a broker dealer is?

A BD is typically a firm in the business of buying and selling securities for itself and others. BDs must register with the SEC. When acting as a broker (stock or mutual fund broker), a BD executes orders on behalf of his/her clients (consumers).

Have you heard of Merrill Lynch, A.G. Edwards, LPL Financial, Raymond James Financial Services, Inc., AXA Advisors LLC, Northwestern Mutual, or Waterstone Financial Group?

There are literally hundreds of BDs out there.

In essence, what a BD does is license advisors to sell securities and clear them (sell them) through the BD. As you can imagine, the liability that goes along with being a BD is significant.

As you'll see when you read my bio information in the upcoming pages, I have quite a diverse background; and at the forefront of everything I do, I try to put the client's or the consumer's interest first.

BDs in my professional opinion are NOT about putting the client first. Most of them are about 1) gathering assets under management and 2) avoiding lawsuits.

Why do I bring this up and why should you care?

It's pretty simple; the alternative wealth-building tools you'll read about in this book are **forbidden** tools by many, if not the majority, of the BDs. When you learn of the power and protective nature of the wealth-building tools I'll be discussing in this book, the fact that many BDs **forbid** their advisors from dealing with them will outrage you.

The tools I will be discussing, for the most part, do not provide an asset under management fee. Therefore, if a securities licensed advisor counsels a client to position money in these tools, the BD does not make much, if any money, and certainly is not set up to make a trail of fees on the money over the next many years.

Also, most BDs do not understand the value of the tools I will be discussing in this book; and it is my opinion that, because they do not understand these tools, they see them as causing potential litigation when sold by their licensed advisors (which makes sense since the BD does not educate the advisors on these products).

NO BD OR BROKER DISCLOSURE

What really gets me on my high horse with the hard core money under management type of advisor is that most DO NOT disclose to their clients that their BD **forbids** them from discussing and selling the wealth-building tools I will cover in this book.

Let me just give you an example that should truly outrage you.

(i) You are going to learn about in this book two very powerful and protective wealth-building tools. The general features of these tools are that they **do not let your account values decline** when the stock market goes negative and they **lock in your gains** when the stock market goes positive (and one tool guarantees you a 7% rate of return (accumulation value) coupled with a guaranteed lifetime income).

Do you think these are tools that a money manager/financial planner should have at his/her disposal? I certainly do.

Assume you are 68 years old and that you sat down with a "financial planner" to discuss what to do with the $500,000 you've saved for retirement. You tell the securities licensed advisor that your most important goal is to not go backwards in the market and, if possible, you'd like to be set up to never run out of money in retirement.

Do you know what advice you will receive from the vast majority of securities licensed advisors? They will tell you that you need a *"properly allocated asset class of stocks, bonds, and mutual funds,"* for long-term money and maybe some fixed instruments like a CD for short-term money.

If you were given that advice in 2007, the chances that in 2009 your account value would be 50% of where you started would have been significant.

Full disclosure to consumers is a huge issue for me. I write my books in a full-disclosure manner so readers know the pros and cons of topics.

The vast majority of securities licensed advisors DO NOT disclose to their clients that they can't even discuss and certainly can't sell the wealth-building tools I discuss in this book.

Using my example, if the securities licensed advisor had disclosed to the client who had $500,000 to use for retirement that he/she could not discuss and could not sell the tools discussed in this book (ones that protect principal and lock in gains in up years), do you think the potential client would have hired or used that advisor?

No way!

The client in my example would have shown the securities licensed advisor the door and then would have gone forth to find an advisor who could help him/her with the tools discussed in this book.

NOT ALL SECURITIES ADVISORS HAVE THEIR HANDS TIED

Even though I just spent the last few pages telling you my distain for BDs and how they tie the hands of the advisors who sell through the BDs, there are some BDs that "get it."

There are some BDs who allow their licensed advisors to discuss and sell the wealth-building tools I discuss in this book. The BDs who allow this don't usually encourage it, but it is nice to know that some securities licensed advisors can provide advice to clients on what I believe are two of the best and most protective wealth-building tools clients have at their disposal.

I can nearly guarantee you this—if a securities licensed advisor gives you my book to read, the chance that his/her BD allows him/her to discuss and recommend the protective wealth-building tools in this book is significant.

PUNDITS AND TALKING HEADS

One of the reasons I decided to write this book is because I have increasingly become annoyed at the advice I hear as it is being given to consumers today by "experts" on radio and TV.

You're probably familiar with Susie Orman and Dave Ramsey?

Without belaboring the point, many of what I would call the "real" experts in the financial services field believe that Susie Orman gives some of the worst advice they've ever seen on her TV and radio shows and in her books. I agree.

The same is true with Dave Ramsey who is known as the "get-out-of-debt" guy on radio and TV. I can speak to his advice as an expert in the field. I've written two books on home equity management.

One book (The Home Equity Acceleration Plan) tells readers how to pay off a mortgage as quickly as possible using a unique mortgage acceleration plan. You can find out more about H.E.A.P.™ at www.heaplan.com.

The other book (The Home Equity Management Guidebook) explains specifically why it's a terrible idea to pay off your mortgage (vs. building wealth elsewhere with that money).

Dave Ramsey and Susie Orman do not speak about the wealth-building tools you will read about in this book. Why? I have no idea, and it doesn't really matter to me. They are not much different than most average advisors giving advice to clients every day in this country (except they can be seen and heard on TV and radio).

My point is that, with my knowledge of the wealth-building tools in the marketplace coupled with the fact that I'm an insider in the financial services industry, I am in a very unique position to write a book telling readers the "straight scoop" when it comes to discussing two of the most viable wealth-building tools readers can use to grow and protect their wealth.

I, frankly, have been putting off writing this book for far too long, and I'm glad I finally found the time to do so.

I hope you enjoy reading the book as much as I have enjoyed writing it; and as you will see in several places in the book, if you have any questions, feel free to contact me at roccy@retiringwithoutrisk.com or you can go to www.retiringwithoutrisk.com for more information.

About the author

My name is **Roccy DeFrancesco, Jr, JD, CWPP™, CAPP™, MMB™**; and I am an attorney, licensed to practice law in Michigan and Indiana.

I've already told you a little bit about why I decided to write this book, and you'll read more stories in the book which will further elaborate on why I devoted time to this project.

As with any book or educational program, I believe it is vitally important for you to know the details of the author's background. Why? When reading a book which is supposed to help you alter your life to build wealth in a tax-favorable and/or protective manner where your decisions will affect you for the rest of your life, don't you think you should know something about the person who wrote the book? I think so.

Therefore, if you will indulge me, I will give you the not-so-brief history of my professional career and will let you determine for yourself my credibility as an author.

Let me start a discussion about my background by going back to my fourth year of undergraduate studies at Embry Riddle Aeronautical University in 1992. In 1992, I was a commercial pilot looking to graduate undergrad in 1993 and start looking for a job. As it turned out, the airline industry was in a tailspin (pun intended); and you could not find a job anywhere (and if you found one, it was a very low-paying job). Actually, to get a job, you had to pay the airlines for your own training (which usually exceeds $10,000).

Thinking that flying would be a fun career, but not the only possible one, I contacted my parents and asked them what they would think if I decided not to work as a pilot and instead go to law school?

To my surprise, they were very supportive of the move; and so in 1993, I started law school at Valparaiso University School of Law.

While in law school, I decided that I wanted to be a personal injury attorney (you see them typically on the back of your phone books). I had family friends who did that type of law, and they seemed happy and made more money than other attorneys in my home town. Therefore, when taking elective courses in law school, I concentrated on personal injury courses.

When I graduated from law school (similar to the airline industry), personal injury law was on the downswing due to "tort reform." Therefore, few firms were hiring in the area where I wanted to live.

As it turned out, I could not find a job that I wanted; and so in 1996, I ended up coming back to my home town of St. Joseph, Michigan, to practice law with my father, Roccy M. DeFrancesco, Sr., J.D. My areas of practice were business law (setting up corporations), real estate law, a little personal injury law, and a heavy emphasis on estate planning and divorce law.

I was truly amazed at how much Roccy, Sr., knew and was more than happy to make virtually no money while learning as much as I could from him.

As it turns out, I've got one of those personalities where I'm always searching for that next challenge in life. The next challenge was to still become a personal injury attorney. After a year or so of working with Roccy, Sr., I found out that our local personal injury firm in town was hiring (a rare occasion). The firm was founded by a long-time family friend who after an interview process hired me to be their new associate in the summer of 1997.

During that summer, I blew out my knee playing with my dog in the yard and had it operated on by another long-time family friend, Dr. Sterling Doster, and his new sports fellowship-trained surgeon, Dr. Gregory Fox. Most people stop me when I'm going through the twisted story of why I do what I do for a living and ask why I tell people I blew my knee out. The answer is simple—blowing my knee out and having it operated on ended up being a life-altering event as you will read.

On one of the follow-up visits with the doctors who fixed my knee (their office was in Bloomington, Indiana, which was four hours south of where I lived at the time), we all went out to dinner. After a few glasses of wine, the doctors asked me if I wanted to come down to Bloomington to run their medical practice. They said their office manager was getting in over her head and that they'd double my salary to come run their practice.

I told them I could not possibly entertain accepting their offer as I just took a new job with the local personal injury law firm in town. After dinner, I went home and continued to work at the law firm. As it turned out and through no fault of the new employer, I really didn't enjoy the personal injury work I was doing.

Therefore, after working at the new firm for a few months, I called the doctors back and asked them if they were serious about me running their medical practice. They said they had a few glasses of wine that night and sort of remembered the conversation. They asked for a few days to talk about it and a week later called me and told me to come down to Bloomington, Indiana, to run their medical clinic.

When I told the attorneys who hired me at the personal injury firm that the medical practice was going to double my salary, they laughed a bit and wished me well. I didn't expect them to match that offer; and as I said, they were long-time family friends, and they simply wanted the best for me.

When I moved down to Bloomington, Indiana, in January of 1998, my wife was pregnant with our first child and things were moving quickly. The lady who was supposed to train me took six weeks of sick time and then quit. I learned on the fly how to run the medical practice, which took a good six months.

As it turned out, I was a <u>terrible manager of people; but I was a whiz with the finances</u>. Understand that I came out of a litigation practice where I went to war every day with other attorneys on behalf of my clients (especially the divorces I used to work on). Then suddenly I ended up running a medical clinic with thirteen female employees who worked under an office manager who really did not give much direction.

Needless to say, I did a very poor job of managing the staff the first six months. The finances of the office, on the other hand, were another matter. Since I had no faith in the previous office manager, I decided to shop every vendor the medical practice used to see if I could save the office some money.

As it turned out, I saved the four-physician medical office over $35,000 in expenses my first year. On what? Health insurance, malpractice insurance, office supply purchasing, outside professional help, collections expenses, overtime; and I successfully helped negotiate a very difficult purchase of the medical office building the practice rented.

After about six months, I had things in the office the way I wanted them from a financial point of view. While I did not always get along with the staff, I have to give them their due in that most of them were top notch and did a tremendous job in their particular specialty. What that left me with, however, was a dilemma.

After fixing the office financially, and because the staff did not require much oversight from me, I had a tremendous amount of free time on my hands. I could run the medical office for what I needed to do as a manager in two-to-four hours or less each day. Remember, that in the practice of law, I used to have 25+ clients all wanting something from me; and now I was running a medical office with fewer than 20 employees. If I didn't come to work for weeks on end, the office would run just fine.

The physicians at the medical office knew I would get to the point of being bored and thought I would open up a small legal practice out of the medical office or that I would play golf every day. Instead of doing either, I decided to research in extraordinary detail "advanced" planning for high-income/net-worth clients (which were my physician employers).

People wonder how I was able to create three advanced education/certification courses with over 1,300 pages of text and two books by the age of 37. It's really not that I'm any brighter than anyone else or anyone reading this book. It's that, due to the extraordinary circumstances of my employment at the medical practice, I was able to spend two-and-a-half years researching: asset protection, income, estate and capital gains tax planning/reduction, corporate structure, advanced estate planning, long-term care, disability and life insurance, annuities, mortgages, on the list goes on and on.

After my research on a topic, I would write an article on it and get it published in any number of places including, but not limited to the following: Orthopedics Today, Physician Money Digest, Physician's News Digest, MomMD, American Urological Association Newsletter, Today in Cardiology, The Rake Report by PriceWaterhouseCoopers, The CPA Journal, CPA Wealth Provider, Strategic Orthopaedics, General Surgery News, the Indiana Bar Journal, the OH CPA Newsletter, Financial Planning Magazine, and Insurance Selling Magazine.

Then I started doing educational seminars for the following organizations (not an exhaustive list): Indiana State Medical Association, Ohio State Medical Association, Academy of Medicine of Cincinnati, Mid-America Orthopaedic Association, the MI, OH, IN, and KY CPA Societies, Professional Association of Health Care Office Management (PAHCOM), BONES, the American Academy of Medical Management, TX Medical Group Management Association (TX MGMA), Texas Medical Association Insurance Trust (TMAIT), the Michigan Orthodontics Association, the National Funeral Home Directors Association, the Society of Financial Service Professionals, the National Association of Insurance and Financial Advisors, and more.

After awhile, you have enough content from articles and speaking engagements to write a book; so I wrote my first book, The Doctor's Wealth Preservation Guide.

MOVING ON FROM THE MEDICAL PRACTICE

While at the medical practice, I started two separate consulting companies—one company where I would provide advice to physicians and one company to work with advisors who wanted help with their physicians and other clients.

As it turned out, I made enough money from the side consulting businesses to allow myself to try consulting full time. By then my wife was pregnant with our second child; and since the family didn't visit us much in Bloomington, Indiana, we also wanted to move back to Michigan so we could be closer to them.

That's just what we did in the spring of 2000. My wife, daughter, and soon-to-be son moved back to my home town of St. Joseph, Michigan, where I worked with my two companies to help physicians with asset protection, estate and tax planning, and advisors who had physicians or other high-income/net-worth clients who needed help.

The good news is that I was making a good living with my two consulting companies. The bad news is that after awhile I became miserable. I don't want to sound like I was crying with a loaf of bread under my arm; but I was traveling a lot to visit clients and advisors around the country as well as doing several seminars, and I was getting worn out. It's not that I didn't enjoy it; but with two young children, I was looking for a business model that would let me go to their ball games, go to the pool, and work in the yard (although I despise yard work).

THE LIGHT BULB GOES ON

I was in Las Vegas in 2004 giving a seminar for the National Society of Accountants (NSA) when the light bulb finally went on for me. A friend of mine, Lance Wallach (who introduced me to the NSA), and I were out to dinner in between the days of the seminar; and I was complaining to him about how I was making decent money but that I was really getting worn out. I basically had made the decision that I needed to do something else, and I was even considering going back to practicing law (it's hard to even type that and see it in print).

Lance told me to stop complaining and then off the cuff said: "Roccy, what you need to do is to create your own Roccy-certification course. You need the School of Roccy."

Of course, he was making fun of me, which I'm sure I deserved; but he was onto something and didn't know it. Lance had heard me speak many times and read my book, The Doctor's Wealth Preservation Guide. As someone "in the industry," he knew that the topics I dealt with in my book and spoke about at seminars were fairly unique and that other advisors who have or want to have high-income/net-worth clients would like to learn these topics.

Like the day I decided to take the job running the medical practice, that day in Vegas was again one of those days in your life you look back on and see it as life altering.

I went home from the Vegas NSA seminar and thought about putting my own educational program together. I figured I could put the program together with no problem. I had a lot of content and some of the best experts in the country who were nice enough to let me bend their ear on advanced-planning topics. The question was: Could I make a living doing "education"?

I said to myself that it really didn't matter as I didn't want to continue traveling like I was no matter how much money could be made. Therefore, I told my wife that I was changing courses; and I hoped for everyone's sake it would work out. I decided to put together what I now call the only "advanced" education/certification courses in the country where I educate CPAs/EAs/accountants, attorneys, financial planners, mortgage brokers, security traders, etc., advanced planning for high-income/net-worth clients.

I formed my own educational institute with an educational board of some of the country's best experts in their fields.

The three courses are the Certified Wealth Preservation Planner (CWPP™), Certified Asset Protection Planner, (CAPP™), and Master Mortgage Broker (MMB™). Each course requires advisors to read over hundreds of pages of text, take a lengthy multiple-choice/true-false test, and pass an essay test. The essay test confirms to me that the advisors who take the courses not only understand the material but can apply it in the "real world."

I rolled the CWPP™ and CAPP™ courses out in 2005 and have had a nice steady flow of advisors sign up to take the courses online or in person. In 2007, I finally rolled out the MMB™ course.

I'm proud to say that the reviews from those who have taken the courses have been tremendous. I imagine that is the case not so much because I'm that great of a writer of the material but because the material is practical and usable in the real world (vs. esoteric educational material) and because the majority of the topics in the courses are new to those who take them. No other entity in the country provides unbiased education on asset protection, which is the foundation of the three certification courses.

My travel has been severely curtailed as I only put on about six in-person seminars a year; and I get to do what I've found I'm best at, which is to help other advisors fashion solutions for their clients. Therefore, it seems that the move from full-time consulting to educating advisors and working with their clients has turned out to be a good move for me, my family, and those who have taken my courses.

RECENT NEWS

As the certification courses continue to get traction nationwide, I am always searching for the next challenge. I found that next challenge when I decided to form a new society called the Asset Protection Society (APS™) (www.assetprotectionsociety.org).

PROTECTION FROM CREDITORS

I finally got tired of all the asset-protection "scammers" in the marketplace who were luring unsuspecting clients to do business with them only to have the clients find out that the services they purchased were worthless and usually far too expensive.

I formed the APS™ with a handful of other like-minded advisors with one overriding goal and that was to form an organization that would protect the public. It's a tough chore and one that will take time to accomplish, but I believe it is a worthwhile cause.

The APS™ is a place where the public can receive baseline education on how to protect assets from creditors (like the personal injury attorneys I used to work for). In addition, the APS™ "Rates" advisors on their knowledge of what I call "global-asset protection."

My definition of global-asset protection is that anyone or anything that can take your money is a creditor. Think about that for a second. Who is your number one creditor every year? The IRS. Is the stock market a creditor? Sure. Did you lose money in the stock market in 2000-2002 when it lost nearly 50% of its value and again in 2007-2009 when it lost 59% of its value? What about the costs of long-term care? Is that an expense that will take your money in retirement? Absolutely.

Because advisors have knowledge in different areas, the APS™ gives out either an A, AA, AAA, G, or O Rating. G stands for global and O stands for offshore.

I wanted to create a Society that would set the "standard of care" in the industry for how to provide asset-protection advice, and I wanted the public to feel comfortable going to the Society to look for help from "Rated" advisors. I believe the APS™ is such a place, and I look forward to having it grow over the coming years with the help of all of its members and State Representatives.

If you are interested in asset-protection or finding an advisor who can help you, please check out the Society on the web.

THE END

By "the end," I mean the end of my overly long summary of my background. I probably made this section of the book too long; but I figure, if you are not interested in the whole story, you can flip through it or skip it. I know that when I talk with people these days, they seem interested in the whole story so I thought I would put it in the book.

The end of the story is really the beginning of this new book, <u>Retiring Without Risk</u>. As you now know, the reason I felt compelled to write this book is because of the bad advice consumers are being given when it comes to growing wealth in a protective manner. Bad advice from advisors to consumers or consumers having nowhere to turn for good advice has cost millions of Americans billions of dollars.

This book won't solve every American investor's problems, but I am confident that readers who take the advice offered in this book will sleep better at night. Knowing your money will not go backwards when the market tanks and will lock in the gains when the market has positive returns will put the mind at ease for many (and some will choose to use a wealth-building tool that guarantees a 7% return every year (accumulation value) coupled with a guaranteed income for life).

HELP FROM THE AUTHOR

Invariably when you write books, you have a segment of readers who want to get in touch with the author to ask questions. I understand that, and I will do my best to accommodate the inquiries. You can always e-mail me directly at <u>roccy@retiringwithoutrisk.com</u>. I am usually fairly timely with my responses. I will be able to give you a brief response, but then I will probably forward you the name and contact number of an advisor in your local area who can help you.

For those of you who believe you need more comprehensive planning (asset protection, estate, and tax planning), you should consider using the C.A.L.M. Plan. It is a platform I put together for the advisors to use who have taken a certification course. C.A.L.M. stands for Comprehensive Asset Liability Management. You can read about the C.A.L.M. Plan at http://assetprotectionsociety.org.

Again, thank you for buying this book; and I hope it helps educate and motivate you to build your wealth so you can retire without risk.

Roccy M. DeFrancesco, JD, CWPP™, CAPP™, MMB™
Founder: The Wealth Preservation Institute
www.thewpi.org
Co-Founder: The Asset Protection Society
www.assetprotectionsociety.org
3260 S. Lakeshore Drive
St. Joseph, MI 49085
269-216-9978

Defining "Retiring Without Risk"

When trying to come up with a title for this book, I instantly thought of the title "Risk Free Retirement."

As you can see, I didn't end up going with my initial thought.

Why? The truth is that in the financial and insurance fields, regulators are bit uptight and most would not appreciate a title that is so bold to say "Risk Free" (it's not in their vocabulary).

The title I ended up going with ("Retiring Without Risk") will still not be "compliant" for some regulatory bodies, but since I needed a title that conveyed what readers will learn, the title I chose will have to do.

WHAT IS RETIRING WITHOUT RISK?

My definition of retiring without risk may be and probably is a bit different than your definition of retiring without risk.

My definition of retiring without risk means that a significant amount of money is positioned in wealth building tools that will **not go backwards** if the stock market crashes 50%+ like it did from a period between 2007-2009.

My definition includes having some amount of your money in a retirement tool that will pay you a **guaranteed rate of return** (accumulation value) coupled with a **lifetime income you can never outlive.**

It seems simple to me.

However, my definition of retiring without risk is dramatically different than how the financial services industry views retirement without risk (again, the term without risk is not a term used in the financial services industry).

Let me list a few different ways that people attempt to retire without risk:

1) Position assets in conservative certificates of deposits (CDs) or money market accounts.

Aside from a banking collapse, money in CDs and money market accounts are risk free. However, such tools also provide pathetically low yields (that usually do not keep up with inflation) and taxable income every year.

2) Invest in real estate (rental or appreciating).

Real estate over time is usually not a bad investment. When the stock market crashes, usually there is not an immediate affect on real estate.

However, as we've seen, real estate values for various reasons can plummet and certainly when trying to retire by using real estate there is no guaranteed income.

3) Bonds. Bonds have proven over time to be a conservative wealth building tool. However, bond returns and/or income is NOT guaranteed and as you will see in an upcoming chapter, the long term returns of the average bond investor has not been very good.

4) Stocks and mutual funds. It sounds odd to even have this on a list of "risk free" wealth building tools. Actually it should not be on the list, but millions of Americans are directed to buy a "proper mix" of stocks and mutual funds to create and maintain their retirement nest egg.

As we all know, those people who had some of or unfortunately a majority of their retirement savings in stocks and mutual funds from a stretch of time between 2007-2009 <u>lost over 50% of their value</u>.

WHAT IS RETIRING WITHOUT RISK?

Let me re-state: my definition of retiring without risk means that a significant amount of money is positioned in wealth building tools that will **not go backwards** if the stock market crashes 50%+ like it did from a period between 2007-2009.

My definition includes having some amount of your money in a retirement tool that will pay you a **guaranteed rate of return** (accumulation value) coupled with a **lifetime income you can never outlive.**

FULL DISCLOSURE

It is important to disclose the risks involved with the two protective wealth building tools I'll be discussing in this book.

If you are scratching your head and saying to yourself that you bought this book to learn how you could use the tools discussed to retire without any risk, I'm sorry, I know of no way technically to do so.

The most secure way to make sure your money is safe from everything that could affect it is to have it in a safety deposit box at a bank.

However, the bank could be robbed and the bank does not reimburse customers for what is in their safety deposit boxes (actually the banks do not know what's in their safety deposit boxes).

This is a silly example, but my point is simply to illustrate that there is no 100% fool proof way to eliminate "all" risk when dealing with your wealth.

Having said that, there are places we are sure with a very high degree of certainty that your money will be there when needed in retirement.

The two tools you will read about in this book can be purchased from multi-billion dollar insurance companies.

Due to their product designs, your money will be protected from downturns in the stock market.

-One tool will allow your money to grow tax free and can be removed tax free in retirement.

-The other tool will grow your money at a guaranteed rate of return (accumulation value) that will be used to pay you a guaranteed income for life.

To me, the features of these products meet my definition of "Retiring Without Risk."

The caveat with the tools discussed in this book is that the company you purchase them from needs to remain financially solvent.

Many people when they think about insurance companies think of the problems of AIG (American Insurance Group). Yes, it is true that AIG nearly went bankrupt but for the intervention of the American government.

However, what most people do not understand is that one of the only profitable arms of AIG was a subsidiary company called American General (AG). American general (while not one of my favorite companies) focuses on and offers the tools discussed in this book.

The key, like anything when it comes to building your wealth, is to work with advisors who know what they are doing and can help guide you into the best financial tools to build your wealth at companies that will stand the test of time.

SUMMARY

The tools you will read about will, in fact, protect your money from downturns in the stock market.

One of the tools will protect your money from income taxes and capital gains taxes.

One of the tools will guarantee you a specific rate of return (accumulation account) of between 4-8% coupled with a lifetime income stream you can never outlive.

Will the tools discussed provide you a 100% risk free path to retirement? No. There is no such wealth building tool. However, when you compare the tools discussed in this book to the traditional tools the American public uses to build wealth, I'm confident that you will seek out an advisor who can help you re-position some of your money into one or both of the tools discussed.

Chapter 1
Traditional Wealth Building: Does It Work?

I wanted to discuss and illustrate how the American public traditionally builds wealth. If you are a typical American, you know the way we traditionally build wealth has not worked too well over the last 10 years (a bit of an understatement with the stock market crashes of 2000-2002 and 2007-2009).

Let me preface this chapter by stating that there is nothing wrong with building wealth the traditional way through stocks and mutual funds. For full disclosure, I have money in index funds (mutual funds that are very low cost and try to track stock indexes such as the S&P 500). I also have a brother-in-law who runs a 5-Star mutual fund (Morningstar). My point is that I believe in having "some" money in the stock market, and I have a unique resource (a 5-Star fund manager) who I can turn to for information on what's going on in the market (non-privileged information).

That being said, I know for a **mathematical fact** (as you will see) that most Americans would have been significantly better off building wealth over the last 20 years in the wealth-building tools you will read about in this book.

If you had an extra $5,000-$15,000+ a year you could use to grow your wealth, where would you put it?

Let me rephrase that. If I asked you that question prior to 2008 or certainly prior to 2000, what would your answer have been?

Nearly every reader of this book would have said the stock market is where they would reposition money to grow wealth for retirement. That made sense, didn't it? Prior to the stock market crash in 2000, didn't we all think the stock market would generate returns for us in excess of 12% a year (as an average)?

When we went through the first crash in 2000-2002, you'd think that people would have learned that diversification should be part of every wealth-building plan. Unfortunately, the American investor seems to like the action of the stock market and so few decided to use alternative wealth-building tools.

The consequence of having significant amounts of money in the stock market over the last several years has been dire.

Let's look at the statistics:

2000-2002 crash

The S&P 500 stock index lost from the highest point to the lowest point 46% of its value.

2007-2009 crash

The S&P 500 stock index lost from the highest point in October of 2007 to the lowest point in March of 2009 59% of its value.

If you had money in the stock market over this time frame, the previous numbers are a painful reminder of what you've been through.

Not to rub it in, but to make the numbers more realistic, let's not forget that most people invest in mutual funds; and even when the stock market goes down, the funds take out their mutual fund expenses (which on average are in excess of 1.2% a year).

To make it even worse, many people paid a money manager to pick stocks and mutual funds; and most money managers get paid even when the stock market declines.

When you add up the losses in addition to the mutual fund expenses and potentially money-management fees on top of that, it's no wonder that Americans who are trying to grow wealth in the stock market are feeling the pain of that decision.

In the pages to follow, I will point out some of the problems with building wealth using traditional tools such as stocks and mutual funds in a typical brokerage account, IRAs, and 401(k) Plans.

1) INVESTING "AFTER-TAX" MONEY IN THE STOCK MARKET (stocks and mutual funds typically)

When I say "after tax," I am talking about money you take home from work, pay income taxes on, and have what's left over to invest.

Before getting into the details of this section, we need to have a little discussion about how taxes affect money invested outside of a qualified plan or IRA (typically in the stock market). Many readers will know about the following taxes and how they affect annual investment rates of return; but, even so, putting them down on paper will help crystallize how damaging these taxes can be when trying to grow wealth for retirement purposes. The following discussion will be limited to stocks and mutual funds.

SHORT-TERM CAPITAL GAINS TAXES

If you invest your money into stocks and mutual funds and you sell either within 12 months of their purchase, there is a short-term capital gains tax due IF you, in fact, had a gain when selling the assets. The tax you owe on the gain is at your **ordinary income tax bracket**. See the following income tax brackets to determine how much you would pay when incurring short-term capital gains taxes on the sale of your investments.

Married Filing Jointly or Qualifying Widow(er)

If taxable income is over-	But not over-	The tax is:
$0	$15,650	10% of the amount over **$0**
$15,650	$63,700	**15%** for amounts over $15,650
$63,700	$128,500	**25%** for amounts over $63,700
$128,500	$195,850	**28%** for amounts over $128,500
$195,850	$349,700	**33%** for amounts over $195,850
$349,700	no limit	**35%** for amounts over $349,700

*These rates are set to change (increase) in 2011 when the Bush tax cuts sunset.

Remember that we have a progressive income tax system here in the United States. You will pay a tax of $1,565 on your first $15,650 of income. If you earn $63,700, you will pay taxes at the 15% rate on income between $15,650 and $63,700 which would equal $7,207.50. Therefore, the total income taxes due on your first $63,700 of income would be $1,565 + $7,207.50 = $8,772.50.

Therefore, if you "actively" traded stocks, let's say with your online E-Trade account, or you have a money manager who "actively" traded your money in an account for you (actively meaning buying and selling stocks within 12 months), you would pay ordinary income taxes on the gains.

The previous chart does NOT take into account state income taxes which range from zero to nearly 10% in California.

For example, if you had $10,000 actively traded where you sold the stock with gains this year of 12%, at the end of the year, you would calculate the capital gains taxes due on that gain. If you were in the 35% income tax bracket, your gain would be reduced by 35% (meaning your effective return for the year is not 12% but instead is 7.8%).

If you also live in a state with a state income tax (using California as the worst example which has a 9.3% income tax as its highest bracket), your 12% return in the previous paragraph now returns you only 6.7%. You can do the math on the money you've invested based on your own tax bracket.

LONG-TERM CAPITAL GAINS TAXES

If you buy and hold investments for **more** than 12 months before selling them, you will pay a long-term capital gains tax. Today that rate is 15% (although it is scheduled to increase in 2011 should Congress not act to extend the lower rate).

This tax is only incurred when you sell your investments. Therefore, if you do what many professional money managers will tell you to do (which is buy and hold quality stocks or mutual funds), you would not have an annual tax bill like you would with an actively traded account or with stock or mutual funds that create dividend income (discussed on the next page).

STATE CAPITAL GAINS TAXES

As stated in the section about short-term capital gains rates (which are taxed at your ordinary income tax rates), many states have their own state capital gains tax due on investment gains. Again, those who live in California are punished the most. The California short- and long-term capital gains tax rate is 9.3%.

DIVDEND TAXES

If you own stock that pays a dividend (income to the stock holder), that dividend is taxed at your ordinary income tax bracket. If you earn $100,000 a year as your calculated income for tax purposes, you would be in the 25% income tax bracket. Therefore, any dividend received from stocks you own would also be taxed in the year received at the 25% rate.

If you are in the 35% income tax bracket, the dividend is reduced by a 35% income tax. If you live in the sunny state of California, you have the added pleasure of paying state taxes as well on your dividends at the 9.3% rate.

While all this talk about taxes might not excite you, or it may even depress you, it is vitally important for you to understand the impact taxes have on your investments that are not tax deferred.

Needless to say, taxes and other expenses will affect how your money grows; and as you will learn in other parts of this book, there are tax-favorable tools you can use that allow your money to grow tax free and come out tax free in retirement.

REAL WORLD ILLUSTRATIONS-FORWARD TESTING

Too often I see advisors, authors, or pundits use what I call "fuzzy" math when projecting how much money you can grow in a post-tax brokerage account.

I'll show you an example that will initially make sense, and then I'll explain the problems with it.

Example: Assume you invest $100,000 in a brokerage account in an effort to help you build wealth for retirement. A broker might show you an illustration that looks like the following:

Year	Start of Year Balance	8.00% Growth	Year End Balance
1	$100,000	$8,000	$108,000
5	$136,049	$10,884	$146,933
10	$199,900	$15,992	$215,892
15	$293,719	$23,498	$317,217
20	$431,570	$34,526	$466,096
25	$634,118	$50,729	$684,848
30	$931,727	$74,538	**$1,006,266**

Doesn't the above chart look wonderful? By investing only $100,000, you would have over $1,000,000 of wealth after 30 years. It's very compelling.

As I've already stated, when you invest or reposition money in the stock market, there are expenses: dividend taxes (at your ordinary income tax rate due in the year earned), capital gains taxes, mutual fund expenses, and money-management fees. Let's play with these fees a little and see how they affect how money grows in the "real world."

For the following example, let's take a very conservative 20% blended annual capital gains/dividend tax rate on the growth and a 1.2% mutual fund expense on only 50% of the same $100,000 invested in the previous example (FYI the average annual mutual fund expense charge is approximately 1.5%). How much less would you have in your brokerage account in the real world? The gross rate of return in the following example is 8% leaving 5.8% as the net return after taxes and expenses.

Year	Start of Year Balance	5.80% Growth	Year End Balance
1	$100,000	$5,800	$105,800
5	$125,298	$7,267	$132,565
10	$166,101	$9,634	$175,734
15	$220,191	$12,771	$232,962
20	$291,896	$16,930	$308,826
25	$386,951	$22,443	$409,394
30	$512,961	$29,752	**$542,713**

The previous numbers should be startling. When using conservative assumptions, you would end up with $542,713 instead of the $1,006,266 earned with money growing in an account that has no real-world expenses levied upon it every year.

Now let's run the same example and add in an additional money management fee of .6% on the invested money (which is a very conservative fee and lower than the industry standard). The following net return you'll notice is now 5.2%.

Year	Start of Year Balance	5.20% Growth	Year End Balance
1	$100,000	$5,200	$105,200
5	$122,479	$6,369	$128,848
10	$157,813	$8,206	$166,019
15	$203,339	$10,574	$213,912
20	$261,999	$13,624	$275,623
25	$337,581	$17,554	$355,135
30	$434,967	$22,618	**$457,585**

Now the returns after 30 years have dipped down to $457,585 instead of the $1,006,266.

Now let's look at how this investment would have performed if in the last 1.5 years the stock market did what it's done lately which is move backwards 59%. I will take the last example and simply lower the account balance by 59% after the last year.

The following numbers will be very depressing and, unfortunately, very real world for many readers of this book.

Year	Start of Year Balance	5.20% Growth	Year End Balance
1	$100,000	$5,200	$105,200
5	$122,479	$6,369	$128,848
10	$157,813	$8,206	$166,019
15	$203,339	$10,574	$213,912
20	$261,999	$13,624	$275,623
25	$337,581	$17,554	$355,135
30	$434,967	$22,618	$457,585
31	$457,585	($269,975)	**$187,610**

After 31 years of investing, the account value after an initial $100,000 investment is $187,610. That's an effective rate of return of 2.05% a year. While that is depressing, wait until you read the upcoming real statistics for how well the average investor has done over the last 20 years.

I'm going to make a bold assumption in this book which is that I'm going to assume that, when you are confronted with simple math, you can make up your own mind about the validity of the numbers.

The previous examples of fuzzy math vs. real-world math are extremely important as you **critically think** about how you want to build wealth and who you end up trusting to help you build your wealth.

Again, my goal is to have you actually understand the various wealth-building tools at your disposal so you can determine for yourself which one makes the most sense to fund and which advisors you should use to help you reach your financial goals.

INVESTMENT RETURNS FROM 2000-2002

It's funny (sort of) when you think about it. Again, if I asked you in 1999 what you thought the stock market's average return would be over the next 10-20 years, what would you have said (remember that 1999 was before the "crash" of 2000-2002 and 2007-2009)?

Most readers would have said approximately 12% annually.

Let's look at a little five-year window from 1999-2003 and see what the best performing stock index returned.

The following are the returns from the Standard & Poor's 500 index:

21.04% (1999)

-9.10% (2000)

-11.88% (2001)

-22.09% (2002)

28.68% (2003)

After the stock market crash from 2000-2002, were you still of the opinion that the stock market would average double-digit returns on a consistent basis?

How did your investment portfolio perform (tax-deferred or not) in 2000-2002? Millions of Americans lost billions of dollars when the stock market tanked between 2000 and 2002.

While you would think the American investor may have learned something from 2000-2002, it is clear that they did not. Unfortunately, the following are the returns from the Standard & Poor's 500 index from 2003-2007:

28.68% (2003)

10.88% (2004)

4.91% (2005)

15.79% (2006)

5.49% (2007)

I said unfortunately in the previous paragraph because, when the market bounced back in 2003 and then continued to be positive for a five-year stretch, it seems that everyone forgot about 2000-2002 (and, therefore, **did not diversify their portfolios**).

THE MARKET CRASH OF 2007-2009

Did you have money in the stock market from the end of 2007 to the beginning of 2009? If you are like most people, the answer is yes (whether the money was in IRAs/401(k) plans or brokerage accounts). Many investors saw five positive years in a row (2003-2007) and thought the market was going back to its old ways.

As you know, the stock market literally crashed in 2008 (the crash started in October of 2007). As stated earlier, from the market highs (talking about the S&P 500 stock index) in October of 2007 to the market lows in March, 2009, the stock index lost 59% of its value.

In 2008 alone, the S&P 500 index was down 39.38%

Let me put this into perspective by using an illustration of account values if you were in the market in 2007-2009.

Account value in October of 2007: $100,000

Account value in March of 2009:   **$41,000**

Account value in October of 2007: $500,000

Account value in March of 2009:   **$205,000**

As you can see, the amount of wealth lost over this very short time frame is devastating. I imagine many readers are nodding their heads in agreement and disbelief as they read the above listed numbers.

Due to the poor advice being given to the American public on how to grow their wealth, many people have had to put off retirement or even go back to work if they were already in retirement.

Many people have had to reassess how they are going to help their loved ones pay for college (since 529 Plans had their values decimated as well with the stock market crash).

Many people are wondering to themselves if they will ever be able to retire.

Many people are scared and are wondering where in the world they are supposed to position their money for growth so at some point in the future they can retire.

What this book will discuss in Chapters 3, 4, 6, and 7 is how to Retire Without Risk by using two alternative wealth-building tools. Both tools **prevent your money from going backwards** when the market goes negative and **lock in your gains** when the market goes positive.

THE DALBAR STUDY

The best study in our industry that few advisors know about is called the DALBAR Study (www.dalbar.com). Much of this study is free and can be found on the Internet. I'll be using that study as a cite for several of the following pages.

When I say our industry, I mean the financial planning industry. It's sad but true that most advisors do not even know this study exists (and virtually none of the general public knows of its existence). To receive a copy of the study, please e-mail info@retiringwithoutrisk.com.

What is the DALBAR study?

It's a study that illustrates how the "average investor" has done with his/her investments in the stock market over various time frames and compares that to what the stock market as a whole itself has done over the same time frames.

When you read the following material, it will truly blow your mind.

The first chart I'll be discussing illustrates what the S&P 500 stock index has averaged over the last 1, 3, 5, 10, and 20 years. You'll notice that the 20-year average is **8.35%**. That doesn't sound too bad even with two stock market crashes factored into the numbers.

Also on the following chart (next page), you'll see that Barclay's bond index averaged **7.43%** over the last 20 years. Again, that doesn't sound too bad.

EXPLAIN

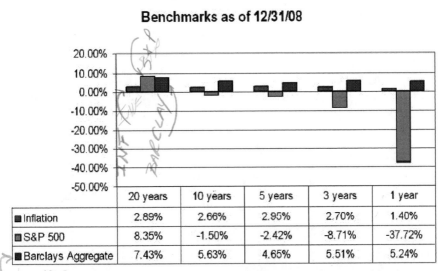

Benchmarks as of 12/31/08

	20 years	10 years	5 years	3 years	1 year
■ Inflation	2.89%	2.66%	2.95%	2.70%	1.40%
■ S&P 500	8.35%	-1.50%	-2.42%	-8.71%	-37.72%
■ Barclays Aggregate	7.43%	5.63%	4.65%	5.51%	5.24%

BONDS

<u>Question</u>: Have you averaged 8.35% over the last 20 years with the money you've had in the stock market? The vast majority of readers once they think about it will answer an emphatic NO!

How can that be? If you've had your money in the stock market for 20 years, shouldn't your returns be somewhat similar?

The following chart from the DALBAR study illustrates what the "average investor" averaged over the last 20 years. What you'll notice is that the "average investor" over the last 20 years averaged 1.87% in equity markets. The chart also lists what fixed income investments returned (.77% over 20 years) and what those who invest using asset allocation classes earned (1.67% over 20 years).

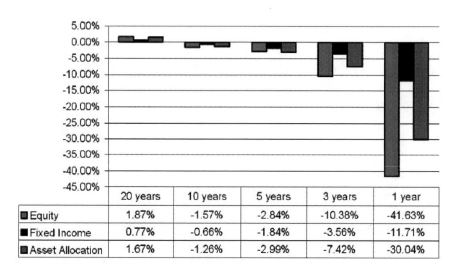

Investor Returns as of 12/31/08

	20 years	10 years	5 years	3 years	1 year
Equity	1.87%	-1.57%	-2.84%	-10.38%	-41.63%
Fixed Income	0.77%	-0.66%	-1.84%	-3.56%	-11.71%
Asset Allocation	1.67%	-1.26%	-2.99%	-7.42%	-30.04%

Now you might be nodding your head and saying that this chart looks more like your long- and short-term investment returns (**1.87%** over 20 years, not **8.35%**).

The million-dollar question is why does the average American investor do so much worse than the overall stock indexes over time?

It's a simple answer that is explained by the following charts. The answer is because American investors are not capable of buying and holding stocks or mutual funds for the long term.

We all (myself included) like to "beat the indexes." How do you beat the indexes? You have to try to "sell high" and "buy low." However, we as an American public are professionals in doing what? "Buying high" and "selling low!"

Also, think about the sales pitch from a local money manager who's been after your business. What's that money manager supposed to say? Let me position your money in the S&P 500 stock index itself and let it sit there for 20 years? You don't need someone to give you that advice (you can choose to do so on your own), and the money manager would make virtually no money if that was the advice given.

Therefore, most money managers will tell you that, of course, they can beat the indexes by buying when it's the right time and selling when it's the right time (even though the previous charts prove that most of the time it cannot be done).

The following chart illustrates that the average stock fund is held in an investment portfolio for less than four years.

Average Holding Periods: Stock Funds

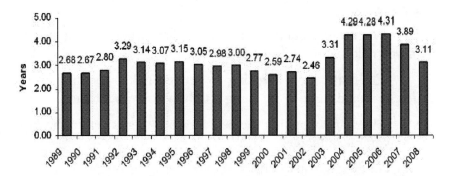

You may think that bond funds should have less turnover than stock funds, but that's not the case as the following chart illustrates. Again, the numbers indicate that bond funds are held less than four years.

Average Holding Periods: Bond Funds

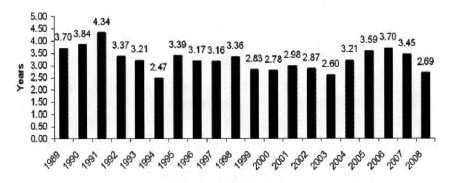

WHY DO INVESTORS DO WHAT THEY DO?

The following are classic reasons you'll see in various books, articles, and in the DALBAR study for why investors act irrationally when selling equities.

"The principles of behavioral finance help explain why investors often make buy and sell decisions that may not be in their best interest, in both the long and short term:"

-Loss Aversion: Expecting to find high returns

-Narrow Framing: Making decisions without considering all implications

-Anchoring: Relating to familiar experiences, even when inappropriate

-Mental Accounting: Taking undue risk in one area and avoiding risk in others

-Diversification: Seeking to reduce risk by simply using different sources, giving no thought to how sources interact

-Herding: Copying the behavior of others even in the face of unfavorable outcomes

-Regret: Treating errors of commission more seriously than errors of examination

-Media Response: Reacting to news without reasonable examination

Optimism: Believing that good things happen to "me" and bad things happen to "others"

There is also one main reason the American investor has a habit of selling when the market is high.

"WHEN THE GOING GETS TOUGH, THE TOUGH PANIC"

The above quote is one of my favorites from the DALBAR study. In essence, the American investor who does not buy and hold has to guess when to get out of and into the market. The study shows that, while investors guess right over 50% of the time, when they guess wrong (in panic sale situations when the market is tanking), the costs of such a wrong decision to sell are catastrophic (as you can see by the difference in buy-and-hold returns over 20 years—8.35% vs. the typical buy-and-sell investor who earned 1.87%).

The conclusion from these charts is that the American investor and their money manager(s), if they have one, are professionals at buying high and selling low. This, over the long term, has decimated portfolios of millions of Americans and drastically affected their retirement lifestyle (if they could retire after the losses).

As I indicated earlier, in Chapters 3 and 6 I will explain how to grow wealth where your money will **not go backwards** due to downturns in the stock market and where the **gains are locked in**.

In Chapter 7 I will explain a different wealth-building tool where you can receive a **guaranteed rate of return** of 4-7+% (accumulation value) and a **guaranteed income for life** you cannot outlive.

As full disclosure, I have no idea what the stock market will do over the next 12 months, 5 years, 20+ years. I am of the opinion that over time the market will be positive and return similar returns on average that we've seen over the last 20+ years. I just don't know when the returns will be positive and, even more importantly, I don't know when the next stock market crash is coming.

IF WE ONLY KNEW

If you knew the market was going to crash between 2000-2002 and again in 2007-2009, wouldn't you have removed your money from the market and placed it in a checking account, CDs, or even under your pillow? Any of the three choices would have been safer than leaving your money in the market.

If you only knew, wouldn't you have waited until 2003 to invest money in the market? Look at the difference between an account opened up in 2000 vs. one opened in 2003.

On a $10,000 investment, the investor who started in the market in 2000 ended up with an account balance of **$9,769** at the end of 2007. The investor who waited until 2003 to position money in the market would have an account value of **$18,284** (which is nearly double the account value over a very short period of time). (The above listed account balances do not take into account taxes, mutual fund expense, or money management fees).

If we only knew, we would remove our money from the market before a crash or wait until after the crash to invest. The problem is that we don't know, and we never will know when the next crash or market correction will occur. Therefore, it is vitally important that every investor have some money positioned in a wealth-building tool/account where there is no market risk of loss (and, ideally, good upside growth potential and tax-free growth and tax-free distributions).

RECOVERING FROM LOSS

Without thinking about it, please read the following question and just blurt out the answer to yourself.

If the stock market decreases by 10% this year, how much does the market have to go up next year to get the account back to even?

Many readers who answered this question quickly without thinking should have said 10%. It sort of makes sense. If your money goes down 10% this year in the stock market, it needs to go up 10% next year to get back to breakeven.

The problem with the math on this is that after a down year you have less money invested; and, therefore, you need a greater return on your money the following year to get back to breakeven. I think the following chart will really be an eye opener for many who lost money in the market from 2000-2002 or again in 2007-2009.

	Traditional Investing
Amount of Loss	% Gain Needed to Recover the following year.
20%	25%
30%	43%
40%	66%
50%	100%

Using numbers from a previous example, if your account value started at $100,000 and lost 59% in one year, would a positive return of 59% the next year get your account back to $100,000? The answer is that a 59% return is nowhere near enough to return the account value to its original starting point.

$100,000 x -59%=$41,000 (new account value after loss).

$41,000 x +59% = $24,190 (leaving an account balance of $65,790).

The return the next year to achieve an account balance back to where it started ($100,000), would need to be an astounding +143.90%.

What the above example illustrates is how important it is to **NOT go backwards** with the wealth you have earmarked to use in retirement.

ALTERNATIVE PLACES TO POSITION YOUR MONEY

If I told you that you could earn returns of up to 11-16% when the S&P 500 stock index has a positive year and has **NO stock market risk** if the index goes negative, would that interest you? I'm sure it would, and you will learn about a wealth-building tool in Chapter 3.

If I told you that you could receive a **guaranteed rate of return of 7%** or more (accumulation value) every year and a **guaranteed income for life** you cannot outlive, would that interest you? I'm sure it would, and you will learn about this guaranteed return/income product tool in Chapter 7.

CDs AND MONEY MARKET ACCOUNTS

There is no section in the book where I will discuss and compare using CDs and money market accounts to grow your wealth. Such investments are not totally useless but are close. The problems with both are that the rates of returns are generally low and what's worse is that the income from both is taxable each year.

Generally speaking, CDs and money market accounts should be used by readers who need access to cash in the short term and by those that want to earn a couple of bucks while they wait to spend the money. They should not be used as a long-term investment tool because there are several other options that provide better potential for growth while guaranteeing principal.

2) INVESTING MONEY TAX DEFERRED INTO AN EMPLOYER'S 401(k) PLAN AT WORK OR IN AN INDIVIDUAL IRA

Large financial institutions and the Federal Government have done a good job over the years of marketing to the general public the concept of planning for your retirement by investing money in a tax-deferred vehicle such as a qualified retirement plan or IRA.

Obviously, the financial institutions are pitching tax-deferred investing to employers and their employees because it's a nice way for them to gather literally billions of dollars under management. Think about it—if a medium-sized employer with five owners and 100 employees contributes $44,000 a year for the owners and $1,050 per non-owner employee (3% of pay which equals $99,750), the contribution to the qualified plan each year would be $319,750. If a financial institution had only 1,000 clients nationwide, the company would capture $319,750,000 in contributions each year.

If the financial institution charged just 1/2% as a fee every year on the money being managed, the revenue generated just from the first year's contribution would be $1,598,750 (if taken out at the end of the year). If the institution kept the accounts and they grew every year at only 5%, the revenue over the next five years for the institution would look as follows (and this assumes the institution picks up no new accounts).

Year	Start of Year Balance	Plan Contributions	5.00% Growth	Year End Balance	Institution Fee Generation
1	$319,750,000	$0	$15,987,500	$335,737,500	**$1,678,688**
2	$335,737,500	$319,750,000	$32,774,375	$688,261,875	**$3,441,309**
3	$688,261,875	$319,750,000	$50,400,594	$1,058,412,469	**$5,292,062**
4	$1,058,412,469	$319,750,000	$68,908,123	$1,447,070,592	**$7,235,353**
5	$1,447,070,592	$319,750,000	$88,341,030	$1,855,161,622	**$9,275,808**

Most financial institutions that market services in the 401(k) market have thousands of clients, many of whom are much larger than the above example.

My point is that there are a lot of companies out there marketing to the general public the mantra of investing money through tax-deferred retirement vehicles such as 401(k)s, profit-sharing and defined-benefit plans, and IRAs. While it can be a nice investment tool to build your wealth for retirement, you still need to **critically think** before putting your money into any vehicle (including a simple 401(k) plan).

IS INVESTING MONEY TAX DEFERRED IN QUALIFIED RETIREMENT PLANS A GOOD OR BAD IDEA?

I'd like you to answer the above question for yourself before I give you my opinion on the topic.

Think about what you know or have been told by your financial advisors, the talking heads on television shows, or other sources. You can invest $1.00 now into a "retirement plan," allow it to **grow without paying taxes** (dividend or capital gains taxes) for 10, 20, or 30 years (depending on your age), and receive the money after age 59½ without penalty to use for your retirement.

When you receive the money in retirement, it will be **taxed as ordinary income at that time**. Is that a good idea?

Most readers of this book will say that it is a good idea. Like many financial topics, **the answer depends**. It can be good or bad depending on your individual circumstances.

Are income tax deferred qualified plans or IRAs "**tax favorable**" because they allow people to grow wealth in a tax-deferred manner, or are they "**tax hostile**" because the money that comes out of a qualified plan or IRA is all income taxed at your current income tax bracket?

It's a good question that I'll help answer in the following pages and with a comparison example in Chapter 4.

INFORMATION ON QUALIFIED PLANS AND IRAS

In order to determine if funding a qualified plan or IRA is a good idea, you have to know what plans you can use and what the limits are when funding each plan.

Let's start with a tool that nearly every reader will be familiar with—the Individual Retirement Account (IRA).

<u>TRADITIONAL</u> AND <u>ROTH</u> IRAs

A traditional IRA is a tool readers can use to allow invested money to grow tax deferred (no annual dividend or capital gains taxes); but when the money comes out in retirement (after age 59 ½), the money is income taxed.

It is important to understand that, while almost anybody can make a contribution to a <u>traditional</u> IRA, only a few are allowed to actually <u>deduct</u> the amount contributed to the IRA. If you are eligible to participate in a retirement plan at work, your ability to deduct IRA contributions is phased out based upon the following income amount:

Year	Single	Married Filing Jointly
2009	$105,000 - $120,000	$166,000 - $176,000

Therefore, if you are married, earn more than $176,000, and are eligible to participate in an employer's retirement plan at work, you cannot take an income tax deduction for funding an IRA.

Roth IRAs are different from non-Roth IRAs. With a Roth IRA, under NO circumstances can you income tax deduct contributions.

On the flip side, a Roth IRA is unique because the money in the IRA is allowed to **grow tax free** and can **be withdrawn completely tax free** in retirement (after age 59 ½).

All IRAs are very limited as wealth-building tools due to the amount of money you can contribute each year. See the following chart:

Year	IRA contribution limit	Catch-up (Age 50+)
2009 and after	$5,000	$1,000

It's tough to "become a millionaire" or substantially increase your wealth when you are limited to contributing $5,000 a year to a wealth-building tool.

Roth contribution rules have a couple of unique twists to them. Due to the powerful nature of a Roth IRA, Congress, in all of its infinite wisdom, has decided that those who could most benefit from its completely tax-free build up and distribution are not allowed to utilize Roth IRAs.

Roth Income Limits

Filing Status	Income Range for full contributions	Phase out ranges	No Contributions allowed
Single	$105,000 or less	$105,000- $120,000	Over $120,000.00
Married Filing Jointly	$166,000 or less	$166,000 - $176, 000	Over $176,000.00
Married Filing Separately	N/A	0 - $10,000	Over $10,000.00

Therefore, if you are married and earn over $176,000 as a couple, you can't even use a Roth IRA.

401(K) PLANS

A strict 401(k) plan is simply a salary-deferral plan that allows employees to contribute a portion of their paychecks into an account in a tax-deferred manner and then allows it to grow tax free until withdrawn. How much can an employee contribute from their pay each year?

	Deferral	**Catch-up**	**Total Age 50+**
2009	$16,500	$5,500	$22,000

As you'll recall from the limits of traditional tax-deferred IRAs ($5,000 in 2009), a 401(k) plan allows an employee to income tax defer significantly more money each year and, thereby, grow wealth quicker. *16% of SALARY*

THE NEW ROTH 401(K) PLAN

A new retirement account was signed into law on August 17, 2006. It is a component of a "regular" 401(k) plan; however, the funding of a "Roth" 401(k) plan is funded with **AFTER-TAX** dollars. This is similar to the Roth IRA but with higher funding limits and no limit on earnings to contribute. Money contributed to a Roth 401(k) plan grows without tax and is **distributed without tax**. (In 2009, the funding limit is $16,500 ($22,000 if over the age of 50)).

PROFIT-SHARING PLANS

Profit-sharing plans traditionally go hand in hand when an employer offers a qualified retirement plan benefit for the employees. Again, the 401(k) part of the retirement plan is a voluntary salary deferral option for the employee. The profit-sharing plan, on the other hand, is usually a discretionary plan the employer funds each year in varying amounts, depending on whether the employer had a good year or bad year (and depending on the makeup of the business and whether the owners in a smaller closely held business are trying to "max-out" the plan).

Profit-sharing plans are non-discriminatory plans with several different ways to test them to ensure that equal or near-equal (non-discriminatory) contributions were made on behalf of the employees.

Combined 401(k) and profit-sharing plan contributions cannot exceed $49,000 in 2009.

BUILDING WEALTH THROUGH QUALIFIED PLANS/IRAs.

Before you can decide exactly where to allocate the money you have available to grow wealth for retirement, I think it is important for you to look at real-world numbers so that you can understand how money can grow in a qualified retirement plan or IRA.

In the following pages, I will show you through simple charts how much money you can amass using traditional 401(k) plans and IRAs and how much of that you get to keep after taxes.

It is important to remember that you will **not** pay annual dividend and capital gains taxes on your investments in such plans. However, when you take distributions from an IRA or 401(k)/profit-sharing plan, all the money is income taxed at your ordinary income tax bracket at the time of distribution. If you take the money out of a 401(k) plan/IRA prior to age 59 ½, you will be hit with a 10% penalty in addition to the taxes paid.

Assumptions: For the following examples, I need to make some assumptions. For the first chart, assume you are able to contribute $10,000 a year through a payroll deduction to a traditional (non-Roth) 401(k) plan. Assume you are 45 years old. Assume the money growing in the 401(k) plan does so annually at 7.5% a year (I know the average investor in mutual funds in qualified plans over the last 20 years has been **less than 2%** (as indicated by the DALBAR study), but I'm going to give readers the benefit of the doubt for my examples).

I will also assume that you will retire when you are 65 years old and will draw down the account from ages 66-84. Finally, I am going to assume you are in the 25% income tax bracket (a very conservative assumption for many given what's going on in our country today) when contributing to the plan and when removing money from the plan.

These examples will use a lot of assumptions. Again, these examples try to utilize "real-world" numbers. I simply calculate the numbers after giving you a full disclosure of how I put them together and will let you determine for yourself if you believe the numbers are credible.

For our first example, using the above assumptions, how much per year can you remove from a qualified retirement plan **after tax** from ages 66-84? **$34,984**.

Age	Year	Start of Year Balance	Annual Contrib.	Withdrawal	Growth 7.5%	Year end Balance	Available After-tax
45	1	$0	$10,000	$0	$750	$10,750	$0
50	6	$62,440	$10,000	$0	$5,433	$77,873	$0
55	11	$152,081	$10,000	$0	$12,156	$174,237	$0
60	16	$280,772	$10,000	$0	$21,808	$312,580	$0
65	21	$465,525	$10,000	$0	$35,664	$511,190	$0
66	22	$511,190	$0	$46,645	$34,841	$499,385	**$34,984**
70	26	$458,389	$0	$46,645	$30,881	$442,625	**$34,984**
75	31	$366,823	$0	$46,645	$24,013	$344,191	**$34,984**
80	36	$235,367	$0	$46,645	$14,154	$202,876	**$34,984**
85	41	$46,645	$0	$46,645	$0	$0	**$34,984**

Let's now make the above chart a bit more real world by throwing in a typical 1.2% mutual fund expense annually.

Age	Year	Start of Year Balance	Annual Contrib.	Withdrawal	Growth 6.30%	Year end Balance	Available After-tax
45	1	$0	$10,000	$0	$630	$10,630	$0
50	6	$60,282	$10,000	$0	$4,428	$74,710	$0
55	11	$142,102	$10,000	$0	$9,582	$161,684	$0
60	16	$253,153	$10,000	$0	$16,579	$279,731	$0
65	21	$403,879	$10,000	$0	$26,074	$439,953	$0
66	22	$439,953	$0	$36,968	$25,388	$428,374	**$27,726**
70	26	$389,071	$0	$36,968	$22,183	$374,286	**$27,726**
75	31	$305,226	$0	$36,968	$16,900	$285,159	**$27,726**
80	36	$191,426	$0	$36,968	$9,731	$164,189	**$27,726**
85	41	$36,968	$0	$36,968	$0	$0	**$27,726**

Look at the dramatic difference in the amount of money available in retirement when you simply add into the mix the average mutual fund expense, which would be charged in a typical 401(k)/profit-sharing plan or IRA.

Now let's change the income tax bracket to the maximum, which would be 35% for federal taxes. The amount you would have after tax in retirement would be reduced from **$27,726 down to $24,029**. If you throw in a 5% state tax, which many states have, the number would be reduced down to **$22,181** annually in retirement. For those lucky few who are in California and have 9.3% as the highest state income tax, the amount they could remove in retirement from such a plan would be **$20,591**.

With most 401(k)/profit sharing plans, in addition to mutual fund expenses, there is usually a "wrap" fee. This fee is part of how a local advisor is paid. If we add in a typical wrap fee of 0.5%, the amount you could remove after tax would be as follows.

$25,149 if you are in the 25% income tax bracket.

$21,795 if you are in the 35% income tax bracket.

$20,119 if you are in the 40% income tax bracket.

$18,677 if you live in CA and are in the highest tax bracket.

Finally, let's look at one more example. Assume that the person in the previous example who funded diligently a qualified retirement plan for 21 years retired just after the market crash of 2007-2009 (**-59%**).

Age	Start of Year Balance	Annual Contrib.	Withdrawal	Growth 6.30%	Year End Balance	Available After-tax
45	$0	$10,000	$0	$630	$10,630	$0
50	$60,282	$10,000	$0	$4,428	$74,710	$0
55	$142,102	$10,000	$0	$9,582	$161,684	$0
60	$253,153	$10,000	$0	$16,579	$279,731	$0
65	$403,879	$10,000	$0	($244,188)	$169,690	$0
66	$169,690	$0	($15,157)	$10,690	$165,224	**$11,368**
70	$150,065	$0	($15,157)	$9,454	$144,363	**$11,368**
75	$117,726	$0	($15,157)	$7,417	$109,986	**$11,368**
80	$73,833	$0	($15,157)	$4,651	$63,328	**$11,368**
85	$14,258	$0	($15,157)	$898	$0	**$11,368**

How's the qualified retirement plan funded with stocks and/or mutual funds working out for this example client?

Not too well. Unfortunately, this is the reality millions of people are facing after the recent stock market crash.

Would this person have been better off allocating some money to an alternative wealth-building tool that offered him/her no risk of loss? Or one that would lock in the gains? Or one that could guarantee him/her a 7% rate of return (accumulation value) and a guaranteed income for life? I think so, and I'll literally go over these two alternative wealth-building tools in Chapters 3 and 7.

Side note: For the previous examples, I used $10,000 annually as the contribution to a 401(k) plan. As you know from the IRA charts, you are not allowed to contribute that much to an individual IRA. If you want to know what the numbers are if you contribute $5,000 to an IRA instead of $10,000 to a 401(k), simply cut the numbers in half. Due to space issues in this book, I've chosen to use numbers in excess of what can be contributed to an IRA when providing examples for wealth building.

RETIRING IN A HIGHER INCOME TAX BRACKET

The theory goes like this: Income taxes today are at an all time low if you compare today to past years and decades. Today, the Democrats are holding majorities in the House and Senate as well as the White House. Our national debt is getting out of hand and will be getting worse as our government implements the largest increase in spending on welfare and other programs in the history of our country. The chances that income taxes will be raised and raised significantly in the near and distant future are significant.

This book is not a political commentary. I personally have no idea what income tax rates will be in 5, 10, 20+ years. What I do know is that we've seen quite a variance over the last 30+ years.

Here are the TOP tax brackets for select years from the past.

1965	70% above $200,000
1980	70% above $212,000
1986	50% above $171,580
1988	28% above $29,750
1991	31% above $82,150
1993	39.6% above $250,000
2003	35% above $311,950
2007	35% above $349,700

I actually never looked up the history on personal income tax brackets until I started doing research for this book. After looking at the numbers myself, I found them to be very interesting.

What I can say personally is that I'm glad I was not a working American in the early 80's, 70's and 60's. While I might not be in the top tax bracket myself (something to aspire to), the taxes seem obnoxious.

While it is not technically correct to say that we have lower personal income taxes than at any other time in our country's history, we certainly are in a period in which income taxes are lower on average than any other time in the modern history of our country.

Does that mean taxes will be going up any time soon? Not in and of itself, but it certainly seems likely. If you want my guess, I believe income taxes will be going up over the next several years and that the increases could be quite significant.

ROTH 401(k) PLANS (a further discussion)

I believe it is important for all readers to learn about Roth 401(k) plans. However, they are not offered by most employers at this time and, therefore, I did not want to take up several pages in this book going over the numbers.

Having said that, I created a multi-page summary on Roth 401(k) plans where the ultimate conclusion is that they are better wealth-building tools than traditional 401(k) Plans (just as Roth IRAs are better wealth-building tools than tax-deferred IRAs).

To obtain a copy of my multi-page summary on Roth 401(k) plans, please e-mail info@retiringwithoutrisk.com; and I will e-mail you a copy of it in PDF format.

EMPLOYER-MATCHING CONTRIBUTIONS

What you'll find out in Chapter 4 is that funding an income-tax deferred qualified retirement plan, for most, may not be the "best" tool for many readers to grow wealth for retirement. Having said that, if an employer is willing to match your contributions to a 401(k) plan, that is going to be tough to beat as a wealth-building tool (especially if you are allowed to reposition the money in your qualified plan as you get older into the wealth-building tool I will discuss in Chapters 6 and 7).

(I'm also aware of the statistics that show that, not only are employers doing away with matching contributions, but many are doing away with them altogether. Notwithstanding that fact, some readers of this book will work for employers who make matching contributions, and I wanted to discuss it).

What other investment in the world can you put in $1.00 and have an account balance of $2.00 with the employer match? However, the match sometimes comes with a caveat, which is that the employee must "vest" in the match or contribution by the employer. To vest, employees usually need to stay employed with the company for three years or so, depending on the structure of the retirement plan.

I could give you several charts showing you the real-world math. However, because a 100% return on your money in the first year of an investment is an obvious benefit you cannot find elsewhere, I'll just state that, if your employer offers a match, you should do everything in your power to contribute to the plan at least up to the amount of the match.

QUESTIONS TO ANSWER WHEN CONSIDERING FUNDING AN INCOME TAX DEFERRED PLAN

Now that you know how much you can contribute to various qualified plans and IRAs, you need to look at the variables that will affect your ability and decision to contribute to such plans.

The following are questions you'll want to answer when deciding if it is a good or bad idea to fund a qualified plan.

1) Do you have money you do not need to take home to live on?

If you don't think you have any extra money to fund into an IRA or 401(k) plan but own a home with a 15-30 year conventional mortgage, then you may still be in a position to raise money to grow wealth. To learn more about how to raise money to grow your wealth without changing your lifestyle, you should consider reading my book titled: <u>The Home Equity Management Guidebook</u>.

Most readers of this book will have the means to income tax defer some amount of money into a qualified plan or IRA or other wealth-building tool if they so choose to do so.

If you have extra money you do not need to take home and pay your bills or buy your toys, then you can choose to income tax defer that money into a qualified retirement plan or IRA.

How do you determine if you have surplus income to defer into a qualified plan or IRA? You can fill out the following form, which will tell you if you have supplemental income that you can defer into such a qualified retirement plan or IRA.

Critical Capital Mass Worksheet

A worksheet to determine how much you can contribute to a tax-deferred plan

1) Estimate your annual living expenses (food, clothing, travel, entertainment, automobile, rent, college funding, mortgages (for your mortgage, calculate the costs after subtracting out the tax savings resulting from the income tax deduction on your personal taxes), etc…)

Living Expenses (after tax) $_____(a)

2) Divide your annual living costs by sixty percent (.60) to calculate how much taxable income you need to take home each month to pay your living expenses.

Living Expenses (a) $_____ ÷ .6 = $_____(b)

3) Estimate your "net" practice or business income after all expenses (do not deduct your personal income (this number should be your take-home income before income taxes and matching payroll taxes)).

$_____(c)

4) Calculate your total pre-tax income.

Pre-tax income from business (c) $_____

Any outside pre-tax income (rents, speaking fees) $_____

Spouse's pre-tax income $_____

Total pre-tax income (add the above three) $_____ (d)

5) Subtract living expenses from pre-tax income

Total annual pre-tax income (d) $_____

Minus annual living expenses (b) $_____

"Surplus" pre-tax earnings   (d) - (b) $_____(e)

6) Multiply the "surplus" pre-tax income by 40% (or your current income tax bracket) to calculate estimated annual losses due to unnecessary income taxes.

$_____ (e) X 40% = $_____

2) Does your employer have a retirement plan; and, if so, does the employer make **matching contributions** for money you contribute to the 401(k) plan?

As stated earlier, if your employer has a matching program, you need to strongly consider contributing your own money to the plan up to the amount that the employer will match.

3) **You need to determine if funding a "tax-deferred" qualified plan or IRA is the "best" wealth-building tool for you. And, if not, what are better alternatives**?

A good portion of this book revolves around educating readers about the "best" place to grow wealth for retirement in the most tax-favorable and protective-manner possible.

For many readers, that "best" place will not be a tax-hostile 401(k) plan where most investors will use mutual funds as the investment tool of choice and subject their money to 100% risk in the stock market.

As you will read in Chapter 3, there are alternative wealth-building tools where once funded money can **grow tax free** and **come out tax free** in retirement (while at the same time **principally protecting** your money from **downturns in the stock market**).

If I wanted to sound like a real marketer, I'd tell you that when you read Chapter 3, you'll learn the "secrets the wealthy" use to grow their wealth. Since I'm an educator and not a salesman, I'll simply state that what you'll read in Chapter 3 will be eye opening and new to most readers and many of their current list of trusted advisors.

3) DO NOTHING

I give multiple seminars around the country each year where I teach CPAs/EAs/accountants, attorneys, financial planners, insurance agents, mortgage brokers, etc., how to provide the best advice possible to their clients. I cover asset-protection planning, income, capital gains and estate tax planning, long-term care insurance, life insurance, annuities, and on and on. I have over 1,300 pages of text that cover three certification courses that are offered through The Wealth Preservation Institute.

Out of all the hours of pure education at the seminars, there is one story I tell over and over. That story is the one of the **Scorpion and the Frog**.

I tell the story in my seminars every time and then refer to scorpions several times throughout the seminar. If you will allow me, I will tell that story here also because it is entertaining and because I think it will drive home the point that we are all scorpions in many ways; and this is NOT something that is helpful when advisors give advice to clients for how to build the most secure and tax-favorable retirement nest egg.

And so the story goes.....A frog and a scorpion are sitting on the side of the river.

The scorpion says to the frog, "Would you let me get on your back and give me a ride to the other side of the river?"

The frog looks at the scorpion and says, "I can't do that. You'll sting me half way across. I'll die from the sting, and you'll drown."

The scorpion says, "That makes no sense. Why would I sting you when that would mean I'd also be killing myself?"

The frog agreed that it made no sense, and so he allowed the scorpion to hop on his back; and they started across the river.

Half way across, guess what happened? That's right; the scorpion stung the frog.

As the frog was dying and about ready to go under for the last time, he looked up at the scorpion and said, "Why did you sting me? Now we are both going to die."

The scorpion looked at the frog and said, "I did it because I'm a scorpion and that's what I do" (meaning scorpions sting no matter what).

DO YOU KNOW ANY SCORPIONS?

Let me name a few and see if you agree with me.

-<u>New or used car salesperson</u>. Have you ever heard a car salesperson tell you that you would be better off fixing your car instead of buying a new or used car?

-<u>Personal Injury (PI) attorney</u>. Even if you have never had a need for a PI attorney, can you imagine visiting one after being in a car accident in which you were injured (where the injuries were caused from the negligence of others) and having the attorney tell you that you should not sue the person who hit you? Rarely does this happen because PI attorneys only get paid when they help clients sue and collect damages.

-<u>Stockbroker</u>. If you go to a stockbroker and ask them what the best way is to grow your wealth, what do you think their answer is going to be? Invest in real estate? No, they are scorpions; they will typically recommend that you invest your money in stocks and mutual funds.

-<u>Life insurance salesperson</u>. Have you ever talked to a life insurance agent before? If you have, you know that their answer to every one of your problems can be solved by buying a life insurance policy from him/her.

-<u>Annuity salesperson</u>. If you seek out financial/estate planning advice from someone who sells annuities, what are they going to recommend? Stocks and mutual funds? No. Annuities.

I'm being bit facetious with all of my previous examples, and I'm doing so to help illustrate my point and to help readers **think more critically** when getting advice from an advisor who is not client focused and/or not well rounded with their knowledge.

I'm poking fun at the aforementioned advisors to drive home a point. Also, for the record, I used to be a PI attorney; and I am also licensed to sell life insurance and annuities.

Many readers of this book will be given the book by a trusted advisor or an advisor who is trying to become someone's trusted advisor.

The chances are significant that such an advisor has not only read the book him/herself but also believes in the advice I give readers in the book. This in and of itself should give readers a good feeling about the advisor.

Why? Because I make the following offer to all readers of this book: If you have any questions about the book or the advice that an advisor is giving you about subjects covered in the book, please e-mail me (roccy@retiringwithoutrisk.org) or give me a call (direct line 269-216-9978); and I'd be happy to answer your questions. That includes asking questions about the advisor's advice who gave you the book.

Since I do not take on personal clients anymore (I refer them out to advisors I train and believe will do a good job), I'm not a threat to advisors who give clients or perspective clients my book. Having said that, advisors who hand out my book as an educational tool know they better go way out of their way to give the most compliant advice possible and advice that is in the client's best interest and not that of the advisor.

Believe me, the last thing an advisor wants is a client calling me after receiving his/her advice and wondering why the advice does not track what I discuss in my book.

DO NOTHING

The reason I started talking about "The Scorpion and the Frog" was to get readers ready for the admission that we all must make some time in our lives, i.e., that we do nothing most of the time instead of the something we know we should be doing.

When most people are trying to decide about doing something out of the ordinary or something that is difficult, they lean towards DOING NOTHING. I know I've done the same many times throughout my life. It is so easy to do nothing instead of doing something—even if we know in our heart that doing something is the "right" thing to do.

Let me give you some examples that may seem silly, but I think you'll agree that they prove my point.

I'm going to ask you some questions, and you say to yourself whether you would do nothing or do something.

-Cut the grass/lawn, which has not been cut in over a week, or continue to sit on the couch and watch the ballgame or other favorite TV show.

<u>Answer</u>: Do nothing and watch the game.

-Clean the house now or do whatever else you happen to be doing at any given time.

<u>Answer</u>: Do nothing or in this case anything else besides what you should be doing (cleaning the house).

-Plan out your estate plan (which usually includes going to visit an estate planning attorney) or do nothing.

<u>Answer</u>: The vast majority of readers know they need to start, complete, or update their estate plans but instead do nothing.

-Be proactive in building your wealth starting NOW.

<u>Answer</u>: Most readers do not know how or the best ways to grow their wealth. Because of that lack of knowledge and fear of doing the wrong thing, readers usually do nothing.

MOTIVATION AND EDUCATION

My goal with this chapter is to educate you in a manner so that you really understand the risks associated with growing your money the traditional way (stocks/mutual funds).

While the stock market has and most certainly will continue to increase its value over time, the problem we all face is when will it increase and when will it crash like it did <u>59%</u> recently in a very short period of time.

My goal with this book is to explain and illustrate to you the power of two alternative wealth-building tools that have **principal protection** so your money will **not go backwards** due to negative market rates of return.

My goal with this chapter is to help you realize that, even though buying and holding stocks and/or mutual funds has worked well over the long term, most people have proven to be incapable of having the discipline to do so. The consequences of buying high and selling low has driven the average rate of return for investors over the last 20 years to below 2%.

My goal with this book is to explain and illustrate to you the power of two alternative wealth-building tools that **lock in your gains** in years when the markets move in a positive direction.

Enjoy the rest of the book and I hope what you learn from the book helps you posture yourself to **Retire Without Risk**.

Chapter 2
Proper Retirement Planning

The American public is interesting in many ways. American employees work more hours per week, per month, and per year than any other industrialized country in the world.

France, for example, has committed to a 35-hour work week; Sweden's system is one of the most developed—parents can take 15 months of job-protected leave per child at up to 80 percent of their previous pay. Today, the average German worker puts in about 1,400 hours per year compared to about 1,800 hours for both American and Japanese workers. The average annual vacation allowance across Europe is about six weeks.

Why do Americans work so hard? You probably have your own opinion of why. My opinion is because Americans like to play hard, live in large houses, and really like their toys. Plus, we seem to have the "keep up with Joneses" mentality which drives us to work even harder.

As I think back to my childhood, I lived in a 2,000 square foot ranch with a finished basement. I loved that house and have many fond memories as a child living there. Today, as I drive by that house, it looks so small compared to the huge houses Americans seem to be building these days.

We are a consumption society. We seem to live for the now, and we admittedly (see the various statistics) do not do a very good job of putting money away for retirement. It used to be that we thought the Government would take care of us through Social Security benefits, and that is simply not the case.

The following statistics are incredible (and depressing). They come from a very comprehensive report, which you can find at www.ebri.org (The Employee Benefit Retirement Institute).

EMPLOYER-PROVIDED RETIREMENT PLANS

Over the past few years, a number of changes have been made to the employer pension system. These changes have caused nearly half of workers to feel **less confident** about the amount of

61

money they can expect to receive from an employer-provided traditional pension plan: Almost 2 in 10 report they are ***much less*** confident than they were five years ago (18 percent) while more than one-quarter are a *little less* confident (27 percent). Twenty-eight percent say their confidence is unchanged and 16 percent indicate their confidence has increased (Figure 1).

Change in Worker Confidence Regarding Benefits From Traditional Pension by Expectation of Receiving Benefits From Traditional Pension

| | | Expect Benefits From | |
| | | Traditional Pension? | |
All Workers Yes No	All Workers	Yes	No
Much less confident	18%	12%	29%
A little less confident	27%	31%	22%
Just as confident	28%	34%	18%
A little more confident	10%	13%	5%
Much more confident	5%	7%	3%
Never expected benefits	6%	1%	16%
Don't know	5%	3%	7%

Source: Employee Benefit Research Institute and Mathew Greenwald & Associates, Inc., Retirement Confidence Survey.

Workers who do not expect to receive retirement income from a defined-benefit pension plan (compared with those who do) and those not saving for retirement (compared with savers) are more likely to report they have ***much less*** confidence in the amount of benefits they will receive.

Lower-income workers are more likely than those with higher income to say they are *less* confident while higher-income workers are more apt to say their confidence is unchanged.

Some workers appear to be expecting to rely on employer-provided benefits they are unlikely to receive. Workers are as likely to expect that they will receive retirement income from a defined-benefit pension plan (62 percent) as current retirees are to receive it (63 percent). At the same time, only 4 in 10 workers report they and/or their spouse currently have this type of plan (41 percent). This means that up to 20 percent of workers are counting on receiving this benefit from a <u>future</u> employer—a scenario that is becoming increasingly unlikely as companies cut back on their defined-benefit offerings.

A minority of workers have personally experienced a reduction in the retirement benefits offered by their (or their spouse's) employer within the past two years (17 percent). Of these, few say they have taken significant steps to improve their retirement security in the face of these reductions.

One-third report they are saving more, either on their own (24 percent) or in an employer's plan (8 percent). More than 1 in 10 say they are trying to stay healthy (12 percent). Other actions reported include planning on working in retirement (5 percent), making greater use of financial planning or investment information (5 percent), planning to postpone retirement (4 percent), and seeking advice from a financial professional (4 percent). Almost 4 in 10 indicate they have **done nothing** in response to the reduction in benefits. Workers age 55 and older are more likely than younger workers to report a reduction in benefits.

WHO IS SAVING FOR RETIREMENT?

It's amazing but one-quarter of workers and retirees indicate they have **no savings at all**. Among both groups, the likelihood of having no savings decreases as household income increases, education increases, or health status improves.

	Workers	Retirees
Retirement savings only	21%	27%
Other savings only	9%	8%
Both	45%	41%
No savings	25%	24%

Many Americans have little money put away in savings or investments (See the following chart).

Reported Total Savings and Investments Among Those Providing Response, by Age
(<u>not</u> including value of primary residence or defined benefit plans)

	All Workers	Worker Ages 25–34	Age Ages 35–44	Groups Ages 45–54	Ages 55+	All Retirees
Less than $10k	35%	50%	36%	24%	26%	32%
$10k–$24,999	13%	18%	16%	10%	5%	13%
$25k–$49,999	10%	9%	10%	11%	9%	10%
$50k–$99,999	13%	10%	14%	15%	11%	12%
$100k–$149,999	8%	7%	7%	9%	11%	8%
$150k–$249,999	7%	1%	9%	10%	9%	12%
$250k–$499,999	7%	1%	4%	12%	11%	5%
$500k	7%	4%	4%	9%	17%	9%

I'm not sure what is most startling from the previous chart. I think the statistic that jumps out at me is the fact that less than 10% of all retirees have at least $500,000 saved for retirement.

How much do you have saved currently for retirement? How much do you think you will need to retire comfortably?

The following chart is somewhat comical after looking at the previous chart.

Amount of Savings American Workers <u>Think</u> <u>They Need</u> for Retirement, by Household Income

	Total	Household <$35k	Income $35k–$74k	$75k+
Less than $250k	26%	43%	28%	13%
$250k–$499,999	18%	14%	24%	14%
$500k–$999,999	20%	31%	23%	26%
$1 mil.–$1.49 mil.	7%	5%	8%	10%
$1.5 mil.–$1.9 mil.	3%	2%	2%	7%
$2 mil. or more	8%	6%	3%	16%
Don't know/Don't remember	18%	16%	13%	13%

The earlier states that 58% of American workers have less than $50,000 saved for retirement. Unfortunately, the second chart on the previous page indicates that 38% of Americans believe they need over $500,000 to retire comfortably and 56% believe they need in excess of $250,000. Finally, 18% of workers **don't know** what they need to retire in a manner they deem appropriate.

While you are reading over these statistics and charts, think about your own personal situation and how much you have saved for retirement and how much you think you'll need for retirement (and where that money is going to come from).

WHEN DO YOU THINK YOU WILL RETIRE?

The following charts are also important as they illustrate that many Americans retire younger than they think (and by virtue of the rest of these charts most do so without anywhere near enough money to live comfortably until they die).

Planned and Actual Retirement Age

Retirement Age	Workers (Planned)	Retirees (Actual)
Before age 55	7%	14%
55-59	10%	21%
60-61	10%	7%
62-64	11%	25%
65	27%	13%
66 and older	24%	15%
Never Retire/never worked	6%	3%
Don't Know	5%	0%

Calculated Life Expectancy for Workers, by Gender

	Men	Women
75% expect to live until age:	78	80
50% expect to live until age:	83	85
25% expect to live until age:	90	90
10% expect to live until age:	95	95

According to the 2006 OASDI Trustees Report, a 65-year-old man today can expect to live until age 81 while a 65-year-old woman can expect to live until age 84.

Calculate How Much Money Workers Need to Save for a Comfortable Retirement

Of all the statistics I found, the following are the most comical. We can't help but laugh at ourselves and as an American public when looking at the following chart which illustrates how we go about calculating our needs for retirement.

		Did Retirement Needs Calculation	
	Total	Yes	No
Guess	44%	8%	73%
Ask a Financial Planner	19%	35%	5%
Do your own estimate	17%	33%	4%
Read or hear how much needed	11%	9%	13%
Fill out a worksheet or form	5%	10%	<0.5
Use an online Calculator	3%	8%	0%
Based on cost of living/ desired retirement lifestyle	3%	1%	4%
Other	4%	4%	4%

While the statistics seemed to show that we are confident in what we need for retirement and that we will actually amass that much, generally speaking we are wrong. It's no wonder why. Forty-four percent of those from this survey indicated they **guessed** when coming up with a dollar figure they need to retire comfortably and, no surprise, of those 44%, 73% did no formal calculations.

Only 19% sought out the help of a financial planner. While the vast majority of financial planners do not know how to build wealth (especially by using the tools discussed in this book), using a financial planner is better than doing nothing (although I would prefer it if you would seek out an advisor who is familiar with and helps clients build a protected retirement nest egg using the tools discussed in this book).

Do you expect to <u>spend</u> more or less in retirement?

The following is what the American worker thinks.

	Workers (Expected)	Retirees (Actual)
Much lower than before you retired	20%	20%
A little lower	34%	24%
About the same	34%	42%
A little higher	8%	7%
Much higher than before you retired	2%	6%

I found the above chart to be very interesting. Forty-four percent of workers expected to spend as much or more in retirement whereas 55% of actual retirees ended up spending the same or more.

That tells us a few things: 1) our expenses are higher in retirement than we expect (see the next chart for statistics on health-care spending) and 2) many workers are not putting enough money away for retirement because they do not believe they will spend as much or more than they do with their pre-retirement spending (in other words, many workers will retire without sufficient money to live on comfortably until death).

HEALTH-CARE EXPENSES

As access to employer-provided retiree health insurance declines and potential Medicare benefits decrease (given the program's projected funding shortfall), new retirees are likely to find themselves increasingly responsible for the cost of their own health care, nursing care, prescription drugs, and health insurance in retirement.

What's really interesting about the following chart is that 23% of those surveyed have <u>NO idea how much money they will need in retirement to cover their health-care costs</u>. How can they possibly plan correctly for retirement if they have no idea? The answer is they can't.

Savings Needed to Cover the Cost of Health Care by Total Accumulation Needs

			Worker Total Accumulation Needs		
	All		$250k–	$1 mil. +	
	Workers	<$250k	$999,999	Retirees	Retirees
Less than $50k	12%	23%	9%	7%	31%
$50k–$99,999	20%	27%	22%	12%	19%
$100k–$249,999	20%	22%	27%	21%	14%
$250k–$499,999	11%	6%	17%	12%	2%
$500k–$999,999	8%	4%	9%	16%	1%
$1 million +	5%	2%	2%	19%	1%
No idea	23%	17%	13%	12%	31%

Some of the other interesting numbers from the chart are that workers who make between $100,000-$249,999 think they will need at least $250,000-$999,999 of accumulated wealth **just to pay for their health-care costs** in retirement.

In an earlier chart, 26% of workers earning more than $75,000 a year indicated that they **only need** $500,000-$999,999 accumulated wealth to retire comfortably. From the health-care chart, some of those same workers said they needed $250,000-$999,999 **just to pay for their health expenses** in retirement.

Obviously, something is amiss with these numbers; and the sad truth is that the American public has no idea how much they need to accumulate for retirement or how they will, in fact, build that retirement nest egg.

I'd like to list a few more charts before we begin discussing how to actually build your wealth in an accelerated manner for retirement planning.

Confidence That <u>Social Security</u> Will Continue to Provide Benefits of at Least Equal Value to Benefits Received by Retirees Today

Year	Very Confident	Somewhat Confident	Not Too Confident	Not at All Confident
2007	7%	24%	34%	34%
2000	7%	21%	39%	33%
1997	5%	17%	36%	39%

Confidence That <u>Medicare</u> Will Continue to Provide Benefits of at Least Equal Value to Benefits Received by Retirees Today

Currently Working	Very Confident	Somewhat Confident	Not Too Confident	Not at All Confident
2007	6%	30%	33%	28%
2002	5%	28%	40%	26%
1997	3%	21%	37%	34%
Retirees				
2007	15%	44%	22%	13%
2002	18%	38%	26%	16%
1997	10%	31%	34%	28%

SUMMARY ON PROPER RETIREMENT PLANNING

Based on the previous pages and multiple charts illustrating what the American worker thinks about and is doing to plan for retirement, it is easy to come to the conclusion that the vast majority of workers in this country are not properly preparing for retirement.

Since 95%+ of the people reading this book are interested in retiring in a quicker and more secure manner, I am basically stating that the vast majority are not properly preparing for retirement.

I'm actually being nice in the above paragraph. To be honest, not only are most Americans not prepared for retirement but most have no idea how much money they need to accumulate to retire in the manner they'd like and most do no or little planning for retirement.

Is it too obvious to state that, if you don't know how much money you need to retire and you do no or little planning for retirement, the chances are significant you will not be prepared when retirement arrives and that you will have a significant shortfall in income in retirement?

The purpose of this chapter is two fold. First, when I read these statistics, I laughed out loud and knew I had to put them in the book for entertainment value. Second, and the main reason this chapter is in the book is to help readers start **critically thinking** about their retirement and examine what they are doing now to plan for retirement (and determine if they have planned correctly or need additional help and tools to grow enough wealth for retirement).

Hopefully, after reading this chapter, I have your attention and now can move on to the various ways you can be proactive to build wealth so you accumulate enough money for retirement to live the lifestyle you desire.

Chapter 3
Understanding Life Insurance

One of the two wealth-building tools I'll be discussing in this book is the proper use of a cash value life (CVL) insurance policy.

Before you close this page and skip to the guaranteed return (accumulation value)/guaranteed income product chapter, let me state without equivocation that a properly designed cash value life insurance policy can be one of, if not, the "**best**" **tax-favorable** and **protective** wealth-building tool at your disposal.

When many people think of life insurance, they think of the movie, "Groundhog Day." In that movie, Bill Murray's character has to relive the same day over and over; and during that day, he runs into an old friend who is a "typical" life insurance salesman. By typical, I mean he's obnoxiously pushing about selling his product (one that Bill's character has no desire to purchase).

Bill does everything to avoid the insurance agent because he doesn't want to hear how wonderful life insurance is and how he needs to buy it from the friend.

If Bill knew how **tax-favorable** and **protective** a properly designed CVL insurance policy can be and how such a policy can outperform tax-deferred 401(k) plans and significantly outperform the use of a post-tax brokerage account to build wealth, he would have gone out of his way to sit down with his friend. (Of course, this makes the huge assumption that the friend actually knows the "proper" life insurance policies in the marketplace and how to design them properly to help a client grow wealth (which is a big assumption)).

DID YOU KNOW?

-Did you know that cash inside a properly designed CVL insurance policy is allowed to **grow tax free** and **come out tax free**?

-Did you know that there are policies that peg their growth to the **S&P 500 stock index** (minus dividends)?

-Did you know that there are policies that give insureds **100% principal protection** on the cash in the policy (meaning that once funded the cash in the policy will not go backwards due to a negative downturn in the stock market)?

-Did you know that certain policies **lock in the gains** earned inside the policy?

-Did you know that there are policies that **credit 140% of what the S&P 500 returns** (so if the S&P 500 as calculated returns 5%, inside the policy the return on the cash value will be 7% (5% x 140% = 7%))

-Did you know that some policies come with a **high early cash surrender value**?

-Did you know that some policies come with **FREE long-term care benefits**?

The above did-you-know questions should have sufficiently piqued your interest to read more. I am confident that, when you learn about the values of a properly designed cash value life insurance policy, you will want to explore its use as one of your primary wealth-building tools.

INTRODUCTION

There are many types of life insurance policies available in the marketplace today. I will cover them in this material and break them down into two categories — the "originals" and the "hybrids." In addition to these types of products, I will also be pointing out pitfalls to policies and tricks insurance agents use to make the purchase of a policy much more advantageous.

Notwithstanding the cautionary language in the previous paragraphs, life insurance can be one of the best and simplest estate and financial planning tools you have at your disposal. What other planning tool do you have at your disposal where in day one you can contribute a monthly premium of $500 and have an immediate payout to a beneficiary of $1,000,000? What other product can you use in a supplemental retirement plan that is self-completing?

What does self-completing mean? Three things can happen to you after you buy a life insurance policy. You can live, die, or

and are left with no insurance coverage (unless you have a conversion rider which would allow you to convert the term to a "permanent" policy (the price of which will be very high)).

Annually Renewable Term (ART)

Annually Renewable Term is not commonly used anymore despite its extremely low cost. ART is the **least expensive** type of a new life insurance policy you can purchase in any given year.

The problem with ART is that the policy renews (re-prices) itself every year. While you do not have to go through underwriting to keep the policy for the period purchased, from an economic standpoint, it is like you are buying a new policy every year. The older you get, the more the policy costs. At some point, an ART policy will cross over and cost more each year than a Guaranteed Level Premium policy. The crossover point will vary depending on your age.

For example, let's say you are 30 years old and the cost of 20-year regular Guaranteed Level Term costs $600 for $1,000,000 in death benefit. That means, if you pay $600 dollars a year for 20 years, you will have $1,000,000 in coverage in force for the full 20 years.

If you purchase 20-year ART, the first year's premium would be much lower, let's say $250. That premium would increase each year and eventually would begin to cost more than the GLT. This is the crossover point. After the crossover point, ART will always cost more than GLT.

As a general statement, GLT is always a better option for those who believe they will keep the life policy for the contract term. ART is usually purchased by people who have very little money and need insurance. They also usually hope that in the near future they will have more money so they can buy a GLT policy so they can afford to keep it for the entire term.

What about future coverage if you do not die by the end of the term of the life policy?

You better have the ability to "**convert**" your policy.

The conversion privilege is exactly what it sounds like—a right to convert the life policy into another policy. It is the right of an insured to convert a term policy into a permanent insurance product (Universal Life, Variable Life, or Whole Life) that the same carrier has to offer. The conversion is guaranteed **regardless of health at time of conversion and is the most important element of a term life policy**.

A conversion right is vitally important in case the insured nears the end of the term and then is diagnosed with a disease, such as cancer or other deadly disease, which would preclude the purchase of a new policy.

An insured may convert to a permanent product at the underwriting class of the term product, priced at the client's current age. Conversion privileges differ with each carrier, but, generally, they offer conversion privileges up to year five after contract issue. Some contracts will offer longer periods, but five years is the rule of thumb.

CONCLUSION ON TERM LIFE

Statistics show that over 97% of the term life policies sold do NOT pay a death benefit. What does that mean? It means that 97% of the people who purchased term life insurance will feel like they wasted the premium due to the fact that they didn't die (although they are usually happy they didn't die).

Generally speaking, most people who have wealth or want to or expect to have wealth do have a need for permanent insurance (either for tax-favorable wealth building or for the death benefit). If that is the case, then buying term life insurance is NOT a good idea.

THINGS YOU NEED TO KNOW BEFORE LEARNING/ DISCUSSING CASH VALUE LIFE INSURANCE POLICIES

A "cash value" policy is a whole life, universal life, or variable life insurance policy. In short, an insured pays a planned premium; and some portion of the premium will go towards the "cash value." The premium allocated to the cash account value of the policy earns interest either at an annually declared rate or a rate that fluctuates due to stock market returns such as those in variable life policies or in indexed universal life policies.

1) **Cash Surrender Value** (CSV)

The CSV of a policy is the amount of cash you would receive if you decide to give up or terminate the life policy. The CSV in the early years of a life policy (typically years 1-10 and sometimes up to year 15) is always less than the cash account value (CAV). **A good rule of thumb is that the CSV will equal the cash account value (CAV) in year 10. ***

*This is the rule of thumb. There are new policies in the marketplace which have high cash value in the early years. I will discuss this type of policy later in the book.

The CSV is lower in the early years to make sure the insurance company stays profitable in case an insured chooses to surrender the policy. The difference between the CSV and cash account value (CAV) comes from the fact that the insurance company has underwriting expenses, has to pay commissions to insurance agents, and has taxes to pay.

2) **Cash Account Value** (CAV)

The CAV in a life policy is the amount of money the company actually allocates to an insured's growth account. The cash account value is always higher than the cash surrender value in the early years of the policy. The insured **does not** have access to the entire cash account value until the "surrender" charges in the policy are gone (which is at the end of year 10 in most policies).

The CAV is really what grows inside a non-term life policy. If there are investment returns inside the policy, they are credited to the CAV. Then the insurance company applies its scheduled penalty (surrender charge) to the CAV to calculate the client's CSV. If an insured plans to keep the policy in place for more than 10 years, typically the surrender charge is not an issue.

3) **Policy Withdrawals**

A "withdrawal" of money from a cash value life insurance policy is the partial surrender of the policy. A policy owner will not have taxable income until withdrawals (including previous withdrawals and other tax-free distributions from the policy such as dividends) made from the cash reserves of a "flexible premium" policy (i.e., universal or adjustable life) exceed the policy owner's cost (accumulated premiums). Until the policy owner has recovered his/her aggregate premium cost, he/she will generally be allowed to receive withdrawals tax free under what is known as the "cost-recovery-first" rule.

<u>Side note</u>: An insured's income tax liability is accelerated if a cash withdrawal/distribution occurs within 15 years of the policy's issue and the distribution is coupled with a reduction in the policy's contractual death benefits. In other words, a withdrawal within 15 years of policy issuance coupled with a drop in death benefits triggers taxable income.

4) **Cash in a Properly Designed Policy Grows TAX FREE and can be Removed TAX FREE**

<u>Section 7702</u> of the Deficit Reduction Act of 1984 (DEFRA) and Technical and Miscellaneous Revenue Act of 1988 (TAMRA) (which deals with the Modified Endowment Contracts (MEC) rules).

One of the main reasons cash value life insurance is used as a wealth-building tool is because cash in the policy is allowed to grow tax free and be removed tax free.

To better understand the following discussion of the MEC rules, consider this question: What is the best investment in the world? The answer is one where money can <u>grow tax free and be taken out tax free</u>.

Assume you are a 45-year old male looking to reposition $100,000 of cash somewhere. You could invest in the stock market or in mutual funds. If you do that, you will have to deal with capital gains taxes, dividend taxes, money management fees and/or mutual fund expenses which will significantly hinder the ability of the money to grow annually.

What about repositioning money into a cash value life insurance policy? What if you could pay a $100,000 life insurance premium, receive a $105,000 death benefit, and have $99,000 cash growing in the life policy totally tax free?

What if after ten years the amount of cash in the life policy had grown to $250,000, and you could access that cash income tax free? Would that be a good tool to grow wealth? The answer is absolutely yes; and in the "old days," that's just about what was happening in the insurance industry.

To counteract what was perceived as an abusive use of single-premium, limited-pay, and universal life policies as short-term, tax-sheltered cash accumulation or savings vehicles, Congress passed legislation modifying Code **Section 7702**. This Code section provides the tax law definition of a life insurance contract; and the modification created Code Section 7702A, which defines a new class of insurance contracts called modified endowment contracts (MECs).

The basic difference between MECs and other life insurance contracts is the Federal income tax treatment of amounts of cash received from the policy during the insured's life.

Certain "distributions under the contract" that are not generally subject to tax when received from other life insurance contracts **are subject to income tax** and, in some cases, a 10-percent penalty when received from policies deemed an MEC.

I am not going to go over the code section chapter and verse on MECs. Instead, I'll explain in layman's terms how the MEC rules affect the use of cash value life insurance to build wealth.

In essence, what the MEC law did was to create what in the industry is called the "**7-pay test**."

What is the 7-pay test?

Based on tables and formulas that I don't profess to understand, in order to avoid having a life insurance policy become a MEC, a specific death benefit MUST be purchased from day one of purchasing a life insurance policy.

The premiums paid, what amounts, and in what years drive the amount of death benefit the policy owner is **forced to purchase** in order to avoid being classified as a MEC. The variable in the test is the premiums paid over a 7-year period.

The goal of Congress was to make it more painful to purchase life insurance as a tax-free cash accumulator. To accomplish this goal through the 7-pay test, insureds after the law passed were and are still required to purchase much more death benefit than they want.

If you think about it, insureds do not typically care that much about the death benefit when a cash value policy is used to build wealth. It is a nice benefit for the heirs to have the death benefit; but if we are honest with ourselves, wouldn't we rather have a policy where the death benefit is minimized so the cash growth can be maximized?

If you don't understand what I'm getting at with the 7-pay MEC test, the following illustration should crystallize it:

Assume you could budget $10,000 a year into a cash-building policy over a 10-year period. You also have the money to fund it today with a lump sum of $100,000. Knowing that once cash is repositioned into a life insurance policy it will grow tax free and can be removed tax free, would you rather fund it in a lump sum or over 10 years?

The answer is that you should want to fund it now so the entire $100,000 can start growing in the most tax-favorable environment you can find.

The problem you'll have to deal with in this example is the MEC test.

If you funded the policy with $100,000 in year one, to avoid the policy becoming an MEC, you would be **forced** to purchase $2,190,157 in death benefit coverage.

If, however, you pay a premium of $10,000 a year for 10 years, the minimum death benefit you would be **forced** to purchase would only be $561,194.

The expenses for both the actual cost of insurance coverage as well as the other costs inside the policy are much higher with a $2,190,157 death benefit vs. a $561,194 death benefit.

While it is true you would have more money growing tax favorably in the policy if you poured the $100,000 in all at once, the additional cost in the policy due to the higher death benefit would significantly hinder the growth of that cash value.

Therefore, what advisors usually counsel their clients to do when funding the MEC minimum death benefit cash-building policy is to fund it over a 5-7 year period.

If you have already purchased a cash building life insurance policy, one question you'll want to ask the insurance agent who sold it to you is whether the policy was funded at the MEC minimum death benefit. I'm sure it won't surprise you that the higher the death benefit the larger the commission for the insurance agent. I routinely see policies sold to clients for wealth building/cash accumulation, and they were NOT MEC minimum policies. The agent only makes a few more dollars in commissions with the higher death benefit, but the negative affect of having a higher-than-needed death benefit can significantly harm the life policy's ability to grow its cash value.

All of the life insurance illustrations in this book are run at the MEC minimum death benefit. Also, for your information, others call MEC minimum funded policies as **"over-funded"** policies. In other words, you are intentionally over funding the life insurance with cash where the policy is not designed for a specific death benefit or a high death benefit.

5) **Policy Loans**

When an insured is sold a non-MEC cash-building life policy, the sale, in large part, usually revolves around "loans" that can be taken from the policy "income tax free." There are two types of loans available in most cash-building policies: 1) wash loans and 2) variable loans.

You will **pay <u>NO income tax</u> if you borrow cash value from your life insurance policy** (this assumes the policy stays in place until death).

This is sometimes confusing for the insured. Often you will hear advisors (including myself) talk about receiving **<u>tax-free income</u>** from a life insurance policy. That's not technically accurate as you now know. You do not receive "income" from your life insurance policy; instead you access the cash via loans.

Generally, loans are treated as debts, not taxable distributions. This can give you virtually unlimited access to your cash value on a tax-advantaged basis. Also, these loans need **<u>not be repaid</u>** (the loan is repaid at death through a reduction in death benefit).

After a sizable amount of cash value has built up in a policy, it can be borrowed systematically to help supplement your retirement income. In most cases, you will never pay one cent of income tax on the gain.

The main circumstance you will need to guard against is taking too much cash out of your policy through loans. If you do that, you will run the risk of the policy not having enough cash left in it to pay the premiums for you until death.

Typically, cash value policies are funded over a specific period of time, 5-7-10-20 years. If the policy is "over funded" at the MEC minimum death benefit, significant cash should grow in your policy. After your premium payment period, there is still an annual cost of insurance that is owed in the life policy. This cost is paid for out of the cash value of the policy.

When an insured borrows cash from a life insurance policy, the policy **must stay in place until death** (otherwise the insured runs the risk of the loan becoming taxable). Greedy clients or owners who do not budget well can get into a situation where there is not enough cash in the policy in the later years (and after loans) to continue to pay the internal costs of the policy. If the policy does not stay in force until death, the insured will have to pay taxes on the loans received from the policy that exceed the premiums paid.

To guard against the policy lapsing and having a client risk their loans being taxable, newer life insurance policies in the marketplace have added a **free policy rider** that kicks in when you borrow money over the age of 65-70 (insurance companies offer this rider at different ages). The rider once activated guarantees that your policy will **never lapse**; and, therefore, you will avoid any potential that the policy will lapse due to a lack of cash to pay annual expenses in the policy.

MORE ON LIFE INSURANCE POLICY LOANS

Many companies have created what are called "**wash loans**" to make borrowing from a life insurance policy more saleable. An example is really the best way to explain wash loans. The following is a non-wash loan example:

If an insured has $200,000 worth of cash surrender value (CSV) in a life insurance policy, the insured could call the insurance company and request a "tax-free" loan from the policy. Let's say that loan is $10,000.

The insurance company has to charge interest in the policy on the borrowed money. If loan rate is 8% on the borrowed funds, then the insured's policy is charged 8% interest on the loan and that must be paid every year.

The insured's cash in the policy is still growing but at what rate? If the crediting rate on the cash in the life policy is only 6%, then there will be a shortfall on the interest owed; and the cash value in the policy will start to go backwards.

If the cash in the policy goes backwards for too long, the policy could eventually lapse (which could trigger a taxable event on the money previously borrowed from the policy). Also, to avoid a policy from lapsing, a policyholder can make new premium payments (which is something most insureds do not want to be forced to do in retirement when they planned on removing money from the policy tax free via loans).

What if the insured had a wash-loan option in the policy? If the insured had a wash loan, the interest charged on the loan would equal the growth rate on the cash in the policy. With a wash loan, the cash in the policy will not have to be used to pay the interest on the loan. Instead, the returns on the cash value will pay the interest.

If the interest on the loan is 8%, the insurance company will credit 8% on the same amount of cash in the life policy so it is a neutral transaction from the insured's point of view. The life policy was charged 8% on the $10,000 loan, but the life policy also earned 8% on $10,000 in the policy to create the neutral position.

Some of the newer policies have what are called "**variable loans**." I will discuss these powerful and much abused loans later in this chapter where I discuss equity indexed life insurance.

CASH VALUE LIFE INSURANCE

WHOLE LIFE INSURANCE

Whole Life (WL) insurance has almost become the forgotten child in the insurance industry. Many companies do not offer the product any longer due to the ever increasing demand for lower cost Universal Life policies (UL).

WL is a form of cash value life. In the old days, a WL policy was considered the only "guaranteed" death benefit policy. By guaranteed, I mean that, if an insured paid the budgeted premium, the insurance company promised to pay the death benefit.

Explaining how cash values grow in a whole life insurance policy is somewhat difficult. Technically speaking, whole life insurance companies pay "dividends" to policyholders when the insurer's investments perform well. Unlike a dividend you would receive on a stock or mutual fund, a dividend paid on a life insurance policy is essentially a **return of premium** that an insured previously paid. The dividend is based on the profitability of the insurance company. So, if the insurance company which issued the WL policy did well with its investments and had a profitable year, the dividend would be high.

Dividends from the insurance company are payable into the policy which can either increase cash values or purchase Paid-Up Additions (additional insurance/death benefit coverage).

Part of the profitability of the company comes from charging clients for the premiums paid. Therefore, when your policy issues a dividend to grow the cash value account of a life insurance policy, it really is returning to you an overpayment on your annual premium.

WL policies generally speaking are the most expensive type of permanent insurance you can buy in the early years of the policy. Without getting too technical, WL polices have a more "levelized" cost structure.

For example, if you are 45 and buy a WL policy with a million dollar death benefit, the actual cost of insurance would be X. When you reach age 55, the actual cost would be let's say X times 3; and when you are 70 years old, the costs are X times 10.

In a WL policy, the costs are not the annually renewable term costs (which rise each year) but again are more of an average over your life expectancy. That means in the early years the costs are higher but in the later years (especially when you get over the age of 70) the costs are lower than Universal Life or Variable Life. Because costs are higher in the early years, early cash accumulation is hindered in WL insurance policies.

Whole life is the **most stable** type of cash value life insurance you can purchase (assuming the company you are buying it from is stable).

As I go around the country giving my educational courses to advisors, I always have someone in the audience who is what I call a 'Whole Lifer." I use this term because they grew up selling WL and believe that clients who want to purchase a cash value life insurance policy should ONLY buy WL.

My view on WL is very simple. If you want a stable policy with fairly high minimum guarantees on the growth of the cash in your policy AND you understand that the returns are not going to come anywhere close to equity markets over the long term, then you should look at a WL policy.

With the advent of new universal life policies which have lower expense guaranteed death benefit riders, the need to buy a WL policy to guarantee a death benefit no longer exists.

If you were to ask me if I would use a WL policy to build wealth for retirement planning, the answer would be no. Why? Because I think the equity markets will outperform what a WL policy will return over time. If that is my belief, I should be in the newer indexed universal life policies which have lower expenses and have other favorable features to them which make them much more attractive policies for wealth building.

THE HYBRIDS

The insurance industry, in order to stay on top with current trends, invented new product classes from the 1980's to present day. Since the products essentially combine features from term and whole life insurance, I will call them hybrids

Let's review some of the hybrid products and determine which might be the best fit for certain circumstances. The hybrids are: Fixed Universal Life Insurance, Variable Universal Life Insurance, and Equity Indexed Universal Life Insurance.

FIXED UNIVERSAL LIFE

Developed originally in the early 1980s, Universal Life (UL insurance) combines the low-cost protection of term insurance with a savings component invested in a tax-deferred account, the cash value of which may be available for a loan to the policyholder. Universal life was created to provide more flexibility than whole life by allowing the holder to shift money between the insurance and savings components of the policy.

Additionally, the inner workings of the investment process are openly displayed to the holder, whereas details of whole life investments tend to be obscure and difficult for the policyholder to understand.

The premiums, which may be variable, are divided into insurance and savings. Therefore, the holder can adjust the proportions of the policy based on external conditions. If the savings are earning good returns, they can be invaded to pay the premiums instead of injecting more money into the policy through premiums. If the holder remains insurable, more of the premium can be applied to the insurance to increase the death benefit.

Unlike whole life, the cash value investments grow at a rate which varies monthly. There is usually a minimum rate of return with UL policies, which sometimes can be 3% or more depending on the bond environment, which is locked in upon policy issue date.

Usually, policies issued during long periods of high interest rates will carry a higher guaranteed rate than those issued during or after a protracted period of low interest rates. Changes to interest rates allow the holder to take advantage of rising interest rates. The danger is that falling interest rates may cause premiums to increase or even cause the policy to lapse if interest income in the policy can no longer pay a major portion of the insurance costs (this is not likely to happen in an over-funded, non-MEC policy which has much more cash than is needed to pay the costs of insurance).

For many years, fixed UL products did not have a "guaranteed" death benefit option. Basically, a UL's death benefit stayed in place as long as the premium was paid and the crediting amount on the cash was reasonable. In recent years, UL products have been updated to allow riders that can guarantee a death benefit in a "paid-up" manner similar to the 10- and 20-pay policies of a whole life policy. In fact, some UL policies will allow a client to buy a guaranteed lifetime benefit with a single premium.

Unlike whole life policies, the investment returns of UL policies do not issue "dividends" as a way of crediting cash growth in the life policy. Depending on the company used, the dividends in a whole life policy might be higher than the investment returns in a UL policy and they might not. Both fixed UL and whole life are fairly conservative from an investment return standpoint (although those advisors who like whole life policies believe over the long term a quality whole life policy will outperform a fixed UL policy over the same period of time). Universal life insurance policies are generally restricted to safe, low-yielding investments; and the most common investments are purchased in the bond markets.

One of the major benefits of a fixed UL life policy is the lower cost of insurance. As stated earlier, whole life is more expensive early in the life of the policy (which limits the amount of cash available to grow in early years). On the other hand, if the dividends in a whole life policy grow to the point that there is the same amount of cash in the life policy as there would be in a UL policy when a client is older, the whole life policy should ultimately out perform the UL policy as a cash accumulator due to the fact that a WL policy has lower costs of insurance in the later years.

The question then becomes: Should you use a traditional UL policy for wealth building?

My answer is no; I would not use a traditional UL policy for wealth building. If I wanted a stable policy, I would use a good whole life policy with a company that has a good track record of dividends that have outperformed the bond market returns.

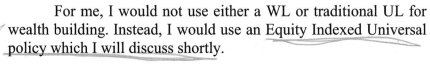

For me, I would not use either a WL or traditional UL for wealth building. Instead, I would use an Equity Indexed Universal policy which I will discuss shortly.

VARIABLE UNIVERSAL LIFE

Variable Universal Life (VUL) is a combination of insurance products and mutual funds. Like its cousin, UL, VUL is very flexible, accumulates cash, and some newer products even offer riders that offer death benefit guarantees.

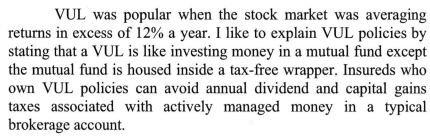

VUL was popular when the stock market was averaging returns in excess of 12% a year. I like to explain VUL policies by stating that a VUL is like investing money in a mutual fund except the mutual fund is housed inside a tax-free wrapper. Insureds who own VUL policies can avoid annual dividend and capital gains taxes associated with actively managed money in a typical brokerage account.

Honestly, everyone loved VUL policies until the stock market tanked in 2000. One of the major drawbacks with a VUL is that there is typically no guarantee on the cash in your policy. Remember, the money is literally invested in mutual funds inside the policy. If those mutual funds lose nearly 50% of their value like many did from 2000-2002 and 59% at the end of 2007 to the beginning of 2009, the cash in your policy will decrease by that amount and more.

Why more? Because in a life insurance policy you have additional loads which you do not have in a brokerage account. I call this the double whammy. Not only do you lose money in the market which decreases your cash value in the policy, but with a VUL, the costs of insurance increase every year.

It is important to understand that in a VUL the costs of insurance are similar to annually renewable term (ART) in that they are very low early on when you are younger; but when you get older (especially over the age of 70), the internal costs for the death benefit coverage are very high. This helps grow cash early and have a high cash value early and really hurts the amount you can borrow later in the policy years and sets you up to have a call for more premiums if the policy does not perform well (especially after you borrow from the policy in retirement and if there are negative years in the stock market).

Owning a VUL in an up market is great and in a down market is a disaster.

Again, the question becomes: Would I recommend using a VUL to build wealth? Absolutely not.

Readers looking to earn 8-10% returns in their life insurance policy with **no investment downside risk** should look at the new Equity Indexed Universal Life policies.

EQUITY INDEXED UNIVERSAL LIFE (EIUL) INSURANCE

As I just stated, many owners of variable life policies have found out that cash values in a variable policy not only go up with the market but they fall with the market as well. This prompted proliferation of a "new" universal life policy, the Equity Indexed Universal Life insurance policy (EIUL). An EIUL policy is a UL policy that has an <u>annual minimum return guarantee</u> but still allows the cash value in the policy to grow at **market rates** every year if the stock market has positive returns.

The policies also **LOCK IN THE GAINS,** which is very helpful in a volatile equity market.

How are investment returns calculated in an EIUL policy?

The vast majority of EIUL products peg the cash value growth in the policies to the Standard & Poor's 500 stock Index (one of the best performing stock index).

When I first looked at indexed life products, I actually thought the insurance companies took an insured's money, applied

X amount to the costs of the policy, and invested the remainder into the S&P 500 index. I thought that was a bit risky, but I figured insurance companies own half the world so they could afford it if they had a few bad years.

In fact, the insurance companies DO NOT invest premium dollars inside an insured's policy into the S&P 500 index. After X amount of the premium dollars are allocated to pay the costs in the policy, the remaining amount of money is used to purchase **income-producing bonds**. The insurance company then takes the income from the bonds and buys the most favorable "**options**" it can on the S&P 500 index.

Explaining "options" is not easy, but I'll do the best I can without boring you to tears. The best way to explain options is with an example.

Assume we are dealing with $100,000 investment. Assume you allocate $90,000 to an S&P 500 index mutual fund (also known as a spider fund).

Assume you allocate $10,000 to purchase "options" on the S&P 500. Let's say with the $10,000 you would be able to buy a "$100,000 option" in the S&P 500 index.

If the S&P 500 is 1,000 when you invested and purchased the "option" and the S&P increased 10% in the first year, what would be your returns?

The $90,000 you invested into an S&P 500 indexed fund would increase by $9,000 to a value of $99,000.

On your "option," you would earn a 10% return on the $100,000 position you purchased. This would return to you your option cost of $10,000, plus $10,000 which is the 10% return on the $100,000 position.

Total assets at the beginning of the following year:

$99,000 + $20,000 = $119,000.

In the real world, when you buy "options," there are costs to the options; and I do not want to get into the exact structure in my discussion for this book. What I will tell you is that, because of the costs and the structure of the options purchased by life insurance companies, the option returns in an EIUL policy are **capped**. By capped, I mean that, if the S&P 500 returns 25% in one year, you will not be earning 25% in your EIUL policy.

Caps on EIUL policies vary per company. Some companies have caps of 16% and some as low at 10%. Usually with the 10% cap products, the company will credit more than what the S&P 500 returns up to the cap.

My favorite EIUL product (**Revolutionary Life**) has the option of receiving a return of **140%** of what the S&P 500 returns in any given year (with a cap of 10%). Therefore, if the S&P 500 returns 5%, the life policy would credit 7% growth on the cash value. That's pretty neat and is a policy for readers who think, like many, that the equity markets are going to be flat over the next 10 years.

It should also be noted that the returns in EIUL policies do not include the dividend income that would normally be paid to an indexed mutual fund.

DON'T FORGET THE GUARANTEES

Talking about upside growth that is pegged to the best measuring stock index is great. However, what is equally as great is the fact that the policies have guarantees in them so your money does **NOT GO BACKWARDS** due to downturns in the S&P 500 index. Every year there is a positive investment return inside the EIUL, the policy **locks in the gains**.

When you couple the locking/guarantee feature of EIUL policies with the potential to earn returns that closely mirror the S&P 500 stock index, you really have in my opinion the "**best**" type of life insurance policy to grow cash for retirement planning.

I know the whole life policy advocates take issue with my stance and that's okay. Everyone is entitled to their opinion. We won't know which policy works the best for 10-20-30 years after one is purchased. At this point, all we can do is look at the numbers of past performance and make an informed opinion as to which life insurance policy will work best to grow wealth.

Here's an example to illustrate how switching to the "new" EIUL policy can save a client significant money. I intentionally used 1999 as a starting point to show you how well an EIUL policy works when the market goes negative.

Doctor Smith in January of 1999 had a variable life insurance policy with a $2,000,000 death benefit and a cash value of $250,000. Because he had his cash value invested in an XYZ aggressive growth fund (which we will assume averaged negative eighteen percent (–18%) from 2000-2001), today his cash value in his variable life policy is $168,100. Needless to say, Dr. Smith is not happy.

If Dr. Smith had the "new" EIUL policy, he would have had plus 2% credited towards growth in his policy in down years; and, therefore, his cash value would be $260,100. (The annual guarantees in EIUL policies differ with how they are credited and no example works for every policy. This example is a generic one I created to give you round numbers which should illustrate the power of an annual guarantee/locking feature).

For those clients using a <u>traditional whole life</u> policy, an example works as well to illustrate how much money could be lost by not using the "new" indexed life insurance policy.

If Dr. Smith bought a whole life policy, the investment return inside the whole life policy could be less than 5% a year (depending on the dividends in the life policy). If he has $250,000 in cash value inside a whole life policy today making 5% in growth every year, he will have $319,070 in five years (these are approximate numbers for illustration purposes). If Dr. Smith used the "new" indexed life insurance policy and the S&P 500 index as calculated in the policy had returns of 8%, he would have $367,332 or about $48,262 more in cash value just over that five-year period by using the "new" EIUL policy.

"FREE" (NO-COST) LONG-TERM CARE BENEFITS

One of the expenses more than 50% of Americans can look forward to paying for is the cost of long-term care (LTC).

Many Americans are tuned into the costs associated with LTC costs because a loved one (parent or grandparent usually) has had to pay for LTC costs.

If many Americans are tuned into this cost and if the statistics state that more than 50% of Americans will need LTC at some point in their lives, then it must be the case that the majority of Americans are buying LTC insurance to protect against this cost. Right?

Wrong. LTC insurance is very expensive, and the vast majority of Americans do not have it (even though many know they need it).

One of the unique features of my favorite EIUL policy is a FREE LTC benefit. How can any insurance company afford to give an insured a FREE LTC benefit? It's actually not that hard to understand.

The insurance company is in essence going to pay insureds money to be used for LTC expenses, and the money is coming from a reduction of the death benefit.

The company is going to have to pay a death benefit when an insured dies; and instead of waiting, the company simply pays a portion of the death benefit early when the insured needs it.

Most people do not think of buying a life insurance policy for the "living" benefits, but being able to receive a FREE LTC benefit is truly revolutionary and gives EIUL policies a leg up on other types of cash value life insurance policies

PROS AND CONS OF BUILDING WEALTH IN AN EIUL POLICY

Cons –

1) If the stock market averages much more than the cap rates for the time the insured has the EIUL policy, the insured would be better off with a variable policy (not very likely).

2) If the stock market averages less than 5-6% in annual returns over the time, the insured may be better off with a conservative whole life policy (unless the policy owner used the 140% crediting method which would have moved the EIUL policy returns to 7-8.4%).

Pros –

1) Your cash is allowed to grow income tax free.

2) Cash can be removed (typically in retirement) from the policy tax free.

3) There is a minimum guaranteed return every year (1-2% depending on the company)

4) The policy does let the owner partake in the upswings in the market, up to 16% with some companies at the time of this writing **(therefore, the policy has better upside potential than a traditional universal life or whole life policy)**.

5) Mortality costs (costs of insurance) are much lower in the later years than a variable life insurance policy and much lower than WL policies in the early years.

6) Flexibility. Unlike typical whole life policies, the "new" EIUL policy is very flexible so the owner can choose when and how much premium is to be paid each year.

7) A FREE LTC benefit (living benefits).

8) Your cash is allowed to grow without mutual-fund expenses.

9) Your cash is allowed to grow without money-management fees.

THE POWER OF USING EIUL FOR WEALTH BUILDING

One good thing about using an EIUL policy is that it protects you from yourself. How? If you'll recall from the chapter on Traditional Wealth Building, from 1988-2008 the S&P 500 still averaged 8.35% (even with a nearly 40% decline factored in for year 2008) **The average mutual fund investor earned only 1.87%**.

The American public is very proficient at buying high and selling low. When you use any life insurance policy with guarantees, you have put yourself in a position **not to go backwards**. Because of this, you have also taken away from yourself the need to panic sell.

I've built up EIUL insurance policies to look like a terrific place to reposition some of your wealth. Keep in mind that with life insurance it helps to be healthy (or have a spouse who's healthy). Also keep in mind that there are annual loads in the policies for the costs of insurance and other internal expenses of the insurance company. These expenses are difficult to quantify, but I will crystallize the benefits of EIUL with several real-world examples which will be compared to other places you could allow your money to grow.

VARIABLE LOAN OPTION IN EIUL POLICIES

As I discussed previously in this chapter, after you build wealth/cash in a life insurance policy, the preferred way to remove the cash for use in retirement is through a policy loan (also referred to as tax-free retirement income).

While everyone in the industry thought "wash" loans were revolutionary as a way to allow clients to more conservatively pull larger amounts of cash out of their policies, when the new variable loans feature came out, that really excited those in the insurance industry.

As you'll recall, if you borrow money from the insurance company from your policy, the insurance company will charge you interest on the loan which is due every year. If the policy has a wash-loan feature, the crediting rate on the cash in your policy will mirror the interest rate on the money borrowed from the life insurance company; and it's a wash/neutral transaction for the insured.

A **variable loan** option allow the insureds to play the market a little by allowing the cash in their policy to grow with the equity markets and borrow money from the insurance company at whatever the fixed interest rates happen to be at the time of borrowing.

If the cash in your policy grows at a higher rate than the lending rate, you actually **make money on the money you borrowed** from your policy.

Let's say the lending rate today in your policy is 6%. Unlike a wash loan where the cash in the policy would be credited with a return of 6%, with a variable loan, in any given year, the insured has no idea what the investment return will be in the policy.

If you purchased an EIUL policy, the growth in the policy is pegged to the S&P 500. If S&P 500 returns 10% in a year when there is a loan on the policy with an interest rate of 6%, the insured has a <u>positive arbitrage</u> (meaning the cash in the policy had a 4% positive return on the borrowed funds).

Conversely — if the S&P 500 goes negative (which in most EIUL policies will earn a return of 0-2% in that particular year), your policy is still charged with a loan where the rate is 6%. What that means is that in the year when the S&P 500 underperforms the interest rate on the loan, the principal cash in the policy will have to be invaded to pay that interest.

Better Potential for Growth

The reason you should consider using a life insurance policy with the option of using a variable loan is because IF borrowing rates and the S&P 500 perform as they have over the last many years, you should actually make money on the money borrowed from your life insurance policy.

How? As stated in the previous example, if the borrowing rate on a loan from your policy is 6% and the life policy which pegs the growth of the S&P 500 earns 10%, you have a 4% positive arbitrage on the cash in your policy.

Historically, the S&P 500 has returned in excess of <u>2% more per year</u> than the borrowing rates used for loans. Will that trend continue? Most likely it will over the long term although as you know: "Past performance is no guarantee of future performance."

It's tough to really get a feel for how a positive arbitrage on a loan can benefit you when you start borrowing from your policy. To help crystallize the benefit, I created a life insurance illustration with wash loans and variable loans to show you the difference.

Example:

Assume in my example that the client is male, 45 years old, and in good health. Assume he will fund $10,000 a year into an EIUL policy for each year until he turns 65 and then will borrow "tax free" from his policy from ages 66-85. Assume the average S&P 500 returns over the life of the policy are 7.9%. How much could he remove from his policy with wash loans and how much from a variable loan where the interest rate spread is a positive 2%?

If the policy used wash loans where the interest rate is 4.25% and the crediting rate on the cash at the time of the loan is also 4.25%, the client could borrow **$38,724** "tax free" from the policy every year from ages 66-85.

If the policy credited on average 7.9% a year as a credited amount on the cash value AND the interest rate is 6%, the client could borrow **$57,421** from the same policy from ages 66-85.

I'm not so sure that it is wise to assume there will be a 2% spread on average between what the S&P 500 returns and lending rates at the time loans are accessed from a life policy. I also do not believe that the S&P 500 over time will return less than what lending rates are when an insured borrows from his/her policy.

Typically, when I run illustrations like the majority you'll see in this book, I manually changed the interest rate on the loan to equal whatever the assumed crediting rate is. In this example, the assumed crediting rate is 7.9% annually. Therefore, if I used a 7.9% loan interest rate, how much could this same client borrow from his life insurance policy? **$46,561** every year from ages 66-85.

I personally have no idea what the S&P 500 will do or what lending rates will be like in 10-20-30 years. What I simply want to do with my illustrations is come up with something that is not over-the-top aggressive and not pathetically conservative.

I also want to make sure readers understand how life insurance agents can manipulate illustrations to make them look very good based on the best of all worlds. I'll do more of this in an upcoming section when I show you an illustration at what many in the life insurance community think the S&P will return in an indexed life policy.

Further Protection

I alluded to an EIUL policy which credits 140% of what the S&P 500 returns every year. I like this policy when discussing the variable loan issue, and I think with an illustration you'll see why.

Assume the interest rate on a loan from a life insurance policy is 6%. In most policies, if the S&P 500 returns say 4.5%, the insured is going to go backwards by 1.5% in the policy due to the fact that the return is less than the interest rate (the client would have been better with a wash loan). If the insured had a policy that credited 140% of what the S&P 500 returns, the insured would have been credited with 6.3% in the policy and would have done slightly better than a wash loan.

Carrying that forward, what if the S&P 500 returned only 3%? The client would be upside down 3% if the interest rate on the loan were 6% in a normal policy but would only be upside down by 1.8% in a policy that credits 140% of what the S&P 500 returns.

My point is simply that the 140% crediting policy <u>allows for more security</u> for the client and better growth for clients who think the S&P 500 is going to be flat for a period of time.

Summary on variable loans

Variable loans are a good option to have in a policy. When buying a policy with a variable loan option, you can choose each year that you borrow from the policy whether to use the variable option or the fixed wash-loan option. The more options the better. Also, if you want to protect yourself when purchasing cash value policies, it is recommended that you consider using an EIUL policy that allows you to move your money when in the borrowing phase to the 140% crediting method.

Conclusion on EIUL insurance policies

If you like the possibility of earning upwards of 10-16% return on the cash value in your life insurance policy in any given year, would like to allow your cash to grow tax free and be removed tax free, would like to take out of your hands the ability and the need to panic sell, and would like to avoid the stock market's negative years with a 1-3% minimum guarantee, then you are a candidate to use EIUL for wealth building.

AVOID THE DANGERS OF LIFE INSURANCE WHEN "REAL LIFE" HAPPENS

What you are about to read in this section of the book is not only critical to you from a protection standpoint, but after you read the next few pages, I guarantee you will know more about the problem I will be discussing than 95% of the life insurance agents in their industry.

I created this section of the book because I had a personal experience with an advisor's client I was asked to work with. What I learned nearly got me sued (thanks to the misinformation from the insurance company I was working with at the time); and as I do with The Wealth Preservation Institute certification courses, I always try to translate what I've learned (even if painful) to others so they can avoid the same problems I've encountered.

Let me just ask you a simple question that I know you will not know the answer to. **What happens to the expenses in a life insurance policy when you lower the death benefit?**

Great question, right? What's the answer? It will surprise you.

Expenses in life insurance policies

When I discuss costs in a life insurance policy, I want to discuss the "**costs of insurance**" and the "**per 1000**" charges.

The costs of insurance are based on your age and amount of death benefit coverage. If you purchased a policy with a $2,000,000 death benefit, the insurance costs are based off the costs for $2,000,000 of insurance. If you had to reduce the death benefit to say $1,000,000 of coverage for whatever reasons (like not having the money to pay the premium), the costs allocated to the actual death benefit coverage would be lowered accordingly (which makes sense).

I like to define the "per 1000" charges as the "other" costs that an insurance company charges the client annually in the policy. Other costs are internal administration costs, DAC taxes, and more. These costs are not insignificant.

The dirty little secret

Did you know that most life policies in the marketplace have a quirk which you won't believe and which can have catastrophic consequences when things don't go as planned?

What quirk? When an insured needs to or is forced to reduce the premiums paid into a cash building life insurance policy and, in turn, lowers the death benefit to reduce costs in an attempt to build the most cash in the policy, the insurance companies **DO NOT** lower their "per 1000" charges.

It sounds harmless, but it's not.

Let's look at an example and see how this policy "quirk" can hurt or destroy the cash value in a life insurance policy.

I want you to assume you purchased a cash building life insurance policy to grow your wealth. Assume that you budgeted paying into the policy $10,000 a year for ten years. If you purchased an over-funded/minimum non-MEC death benefit policy to minimize your expenses and maximize your cash growth, assume the death benefit purchased is $500,000.

Also assume that in year 3 you lost your job, got divorced, or became disabled. Why do I want you to assume one of these three things happened? Because I want you to assume you can no longer afford to pay your life insurance premium. Since 50% or more of Americans get divorced, I do not think this example is anything but real world.

Finally, assume that, when you can't pay the premium any longer, you call the insurance company and tell them to drop the death benefit down to the lowest possible non-MEC death benefit.

When you reduce the death benefit to the new non-MEC death benefit, you assume that you will pay no further premiums into the policy. By doing so, the policy has a chance to continue for some years to come without lapsing due to lack of premium payments (the premiums will be paid from the cash value which hopefully is growing in the policy).

Is it fair to say that one of the first expenses you'll not want to pay when you have a cash crunch is your life insurance premium?

When you tell your life insurance agent that you have decided not to pay the premiums because of financial problems, what will a typical advisor say to you? Sorry, your policy will explode in the next few years; and the $30,000 in premiums will evaporate?

Probably not. An advisor will probably advise you to lower the death benefit down to the lowest point possible (the new non-MEC minimum death benefit assuming no or little future premiums). The theory being that, if the death benefit is lowered, the expenses will be lowered; and the policy will still build cash and certainly won't lapse.

Right? Wrong.

What's the problem with this thinking? The "costs of insurance" will be lowered when the death benefit is lowered, but the "per 1000" charges WILL NOT. If, in the above example, the insured started with a $500,000 death benefit and lowered it down to say $100,000, the "costs of insurance" would be lowered to the costs for $100,000 of coverage; but the "per 1000" charges will be charged as if the insured still had $500,000 coverage.

The end result will be that in a few years after an insured lowers the death benefit and reduces or stops paying premiums, he/she will likely receive a letter from the insurance company telling him/her that the policy is going to **lapse** unless more premiums are paid.

Why do companies NOT lower the "per 1000" charges?

I've been told by actuaries at several companies that the reasons have to do with the costs incurred by the insurance company in the early years after issuing a policy which must be recouped regardless of whether a client lowers the death benefit or not.

What costs? Little costs like insurance agent commissions (which are usually paid up front) and taxes the insurance company pays which are based on the initial death benefit at issue.

Usually the insurance companies spread these costs over the first 10-15 years; and if an insured lowers the death benefit after that time frame, then the "per 1000" charges should be lowered.

Do all life insurance policies have this problem?

No. When I learned of this "per 1000" charge problem several years ago, I looked high and low for a policy that was more client friendly. There are a few in the marketplace, and one in particular that I prefer is called Revolutionary Life. I'm proud to say that the policy has a rider (with little cost) where you can choose to have the "per 1000" charges lowered in the event the death benefit is lowered in the first 10 years.

Why am I discussing this narrow topic in a general public book?

The main reason (as sad as it sounds) is that most insurance licensed advisors selling life insurance do not understand this problem or the fact that there are policies in the market with provisions to waive this problem. Because of this, I think it is vitally important that non-advisors who read this book understand this issue so informed decisions can be made when purchasing a cash value life insurance policy for wealth building.

If you didn't know any better after reading the other books in the marketplace, you'd think an indexed equity life insurance policy acts more like a tax free money market account with no surrender charges and no insurance costs other than a life insurance policy. That is not the case.

For those who are financially stable or have a decent amount of liquid wealth in various accounts, there is not much of a need to have a high cash value life insurance policy with the rider that lowers the "per 1000" charges. Why? Remember there is a slight cost to the riders; and if the rider is not necessary, then you can choose not to use it and build more wealth in your policy.

SUMMARY ON THE DANGERS IN LIFE INSURANCE POLICIES

It's important for the general public to be armed with the appropriate knowledge as to how life insurance policies work. Everyone will want to tell you how an over-funded, non-MEC cash building life insurance policy can be a terrific wealth builder due to tax-free growth and tax-fee loans.

When working with advisors, however, you not only want to know the good about products, you want to know the bad or downside and the options to mitigate that risk if you so choose. Unfortunately, there are few advisors who really understand the "per 1000" charge issue and few who are familiar with high cash value policies.

CONCLUSION ON LIFE INSURANCE

To say that life insurance is a misunderstood tool when it comes to wealth building would be a dramatic understatement. When insureds do not understand how and why a wealth-building tool works, how can they be expected to embrace its use as part of a main tool in their overall financial/retirement plan?

While this one chapter will not make you a life insurance expert, I hope you have learned a few things you didn't know before you read this chapter. I hope now you know the differences between term, whole, universal, variable and indexed universal life insurance.

I hope you understand the tax-free aspects of building wealth in life insurance policies which are designed as over-funded, non-MEC policies.

Since I believe EIUL is the best type of cash building policy, I spent quite a bit of time explaining how the policy works to protect your cash from downturns in the stock market while providing you good upside potential in the equity market (the S&P 500).

If you understand how variable loans work with EIUL, I can guarantee you that you know more about the product than half of the agents selling it.

While many readers think that anyone can get a life insurance license and, therefore, anyone can give good advice about life insurance policies, you now know that there are many variables and nuances to life insurance policies that must be known in order to give the best advice to clients.

Most non-insurance advisors do not try to give advice to clients on the issue of life insurance except to tell the client to purchase a policy with the lowest possible costs with a highly rated carrier. With the information learned in this book, you should be able to have a meaningful discussion with a life insurance agent about the best type of life insurance that is best for you to grow your wealth.

I also suspect that many readers learned that the last life insurance agent they purchased a policy from did not fully disclose the pros and cons of the product or simply did not come to the table with the best product. If you are one of those people, do not hesitate to e-mail me at roccy@retiringwithoutrisk.com; and I'd be happy to refer you to a properly trained local advisor you can contact who can review your current policy to determine if there is a way to fix it or 1035 (tax-free) exchange it to a newer better policy.

Now that you should have a good working knowledge about CVL insurance; I will move on to discuss how CVL insurance compares as a wealth-building tool to funding stocks, mutual funds after tax in a brokerage account, or building wealth through tax deferred IRAs/401(k) plans and Roth IRAs/401(k) plans.

I think you will find my conclusions and illustrations with "real" math very interesting, and I guarantee you it will surprise you and I hope it will motivate you to look into the use of a protective CVL insurance policy as a primary wealth-building tool.

Chapter 4
Funding Qualified Retirement Plans and/or Post-Tax Brokerage Accounts vs. Cash Value Life Insurance

To date, there has been no "authoritative" writing with **real details** on the two questions which are raised over and over in the life insurance and financial-planning communities.

Question 1: Is it better for you to fund a qualified retirement plan such as a 401(k) plan, or is it better to take your income home, pay tax on it, and fund cash value life insurance as a retirement vehicle?

In this chapter, I will show you with real-world math using different variables how much you can anticipate receiving after tax in retirement from a traditional 401(k) plan vs. after tax from a cash value life insurance policy.

Question 2: Is it better to fund a post-tax brokerage account to grow your wealth or use cash value life insurance?

Again, I will show you with real-world math how much you can anticipate receiving after tax in retirement from a brokerage account vs. after tax from a cash value life insurance policy.

As I alluded to in an earlier part of this book, there is no such thing as a "secret" wealth-building tool. Having said that, there are very few who fully understand the power and protective nature of a properly designed CVL insurance policy.

-Keep in mind the statistics from Chapter 1. The S&P 500 index, even with the nearly 40% decrease in 2008, still averaged **8.35%** from 1988-2008 while the average mutual fund investor earned only **1.85%**.

-Keep in mind that the average mutual fund is held for less than four years and that most American investors **panic sell** when the stock market starts to crash. In other words, the American investor is a professional at "buying high" and "selling low."

-Keep in mind that with an equity indexed life insurance (EIUL) policy, you do not lose money when the stock market goes negative; and your gains are locked in after positive years in the market.

-Keep in mind that with an EIUL policy your money **grows tax free** and can be **removed tax free**.

-Keep in mind that with the right EIUL policy (***Revolutionary Life***) you will receive not only a death benefit to protect the family but also living benefits such as a **FREE long-term care benefit**.

LAYOUT OF THIS CHAPTER

This is not going to be the easiest chapter of a book you've ever read. I usually have a good knack for breaking down complex topics into English for people, and this chapter will challenge that ability. Actually, the subject matter of this chapter is not too bad; but because of the multiple comparisons and charts, it will probably be a bit confusing for some readers.

The good news is that the details that support the conclusions are in this chapter, but I also have summaries with just the conclusions. Therefore, you can read as much as you want and read it over a few times to get all the details; or you can take the conclusions as they are. I recommend learning the details that support the numbers; but the bottom line is that I want you to know the outcome of the math, which will be very interesting and eye opening for most readers.

Like Chapter 3, for the sake of brevity, I did not put into this chapter the numbers on the Roth 401(k) plan. Again, most employees do not have the option of funding a Roth 401(k) plan and; therefore, I did not want to take up space in this book discussing it.

I have, however, run all the numbers on Roth 401(k) Plans in the same manner as you'll read in the following pages on traditional tax-deferred 401(k) plans. If you would like to read this information, simply e-mail roccy@retiringwithoutrisk.com; and I'll e-mail you PDF summary that includes Roth 401(k) plan numbers.

The chapter will be laid out as follows when dealing with a particular client (**Mr. Smith**) who is looking to build wealth for retirement.

The following material:

1) Illustrates how much after-tax retirement income Mr. Smith will have available using a **traditional/deductible 401(k) plan**.

2) Compares what Mr. Smith has available from a **traditional 401(k) plan** to what he could receive if he funded a **cash value life insurance policy**.

3) Illustrates how much after-tax retirement income Mr. Smith will have available when funding a typical **after-tax brokerage account**.

4) Compares what Mr. Smith has available from the **post-tax brokerage account** to what he could receive if he funded a **cash value life insurance policy**.

The material to follow will illustrate the economics for Mr. Smith as if he were in the 40%, 30%, and 15% income tax brackets when funding and removing money from his 401(k) plan and when funding and removing money from a cash value life insurance policy.

For the examples in this chapter:

-Assume the client, Mr. Smith, who is age 45, contributes $15,000 to a traditional tax-deductible 401(k) plan each year for 21 (45-65) years and takes distributions from the plan from ages 66-85 (leaving an account value of zero at age 85).

-Assume that Mr. Smith will fund a post-tax brokerage account with $15,000 every year for 21 years and will remove money from the account from ages 66-85 (leaving an account balance of zero at age 85).

-Assume that Mr. Smith funds $15,000 after tax to a cash value life insurance policy and removes money from the policy from ages 66-85 (leaving enough cash in the policy to keep it in force until death).

Because the contribution is <u>non-deductible</u> to the cash value life insurance policy and the post-tax brokerage account, Mr. Smith will have to pay the following taxes on his contribution to either. The amount of tax depends on his income tax bracket. As stated, I will show you numbers for each tax bracket so you can look at the one that most closely fits your situation:

- 40% tax bracket = $6,000 tax

- 30% tax bracket = $4,500 tax

- 15% tax bracket = $2,250 tax

The examples in this chapter all assume a fairly conservative <u>7%</u> investment return over the life of plan.

For a comparison example, Mr. Smith will invest an amount of money equal to the taxes he <u>would have saved</u> had a traditional tax-deferred 401(k) plan been implemented (a <u>side account</u>).

In other words, if Mr. Smith funded a traditional tax deductible 401(k) plan, he would NOT have had to pay the additional taxes listed previously when funding a cash value life insurance policy or a post-tax brokerage account.

Therefore, when comparing numbers for Mr. Smith to fund a cash value life insurance policy or a post-tax brokerage account vs. a tax deferred 401(k) plan, he would have to fund into the side fund $6,000 in the 40% tax bracket, $4,500 in the 30% tax bracket, and $2,250 in the 15% tax bracket.

When most advisors discuss a side fund, they are talking about a typical investment account. When you actively invest money in the stock market (after tax), in order to have a "real-world" example, the numbers must reflect <u>capital gains/dividend taxes</u> on the post-tax brokerage account. The following are the assumed annual taxes on the growth in the account:

- 25% for a client in the 40% tax bracket

- 20% for a client in the 30% tax bracket

- 15% for a client in the 15% tax bracket

Also, when people, including Mr. Smith, invest money in a 401(k) plan, they typically will use mutual funds. For the first example, I will assume only a **.6% annual mutual fund expense** on money inside the 401(k) plan. The industry average is in excess of **1.5%** so this first example will not be terribly real world. Additionally, I will assume no "wrap fee" or money management fee even though many plans have these additional fees.

Alright. Now that you have an understanding of some of the variables (and if you don't, don't worry, I'll give you the charts which show you the answers), let's see how Mr. Smith does with retirement planning using these various plans.

1) How much can Mr. Smith receive in retirement from his traditional <u>tax-deferred</u> 401(k) plan?

If Mr. Smith funded a regular income-tax-deferred 401(k) plan, the following is how much he could receive from ages 66-85 after tax. Remember that money, when withdrawn from a traditional 401(k) plan, is **<u>fully income taxable</u>** in the year received.

Mr. Smith could remove annually from ages 66-85 the following, depending on his income tax bracket in retirement:

- $33,925 in the 40% tax bracket
- $39,579 in the 30% tax bracket
- $48,060 in the 15% tax bracket

As I like to do, I'd like you to be able to see how money grows for yourself. However, for the sake of brevity, I'll only include a chart with the actual math for how money grows and is withdrawn from a traditional 401(k) plan for Mr. Smith, assuming he is in the <u>30% income tax bracket</u>.

Age	Start of Year Balance	Annual Contrib.	Withdrawal 401(k)	Growth 6.40%	Year end Balance	Available After-tax
45	$0	$15,000	$0	$960	$15,960	$0
50	$90,689	$15,000	$0	$6,764	$112,453	$0
60	$383,004	$15,000	$0	$25,472	$423,476	$0
65	$612,979	$15,000	$0	$40,191	$668,169	$0
66	$668,169	$0	$56,541	$39,144	$650,772	**$39,579**
70	$591,611	$0	$56,541	$34,244	$569,315	**$39,579**
75	$464,915	$0	$56,541	$26,136	$434,510	**$39,579**
80	$292,144	$0	$56,541	$15,079	$250,681	**$39,579**
85	$56,541	$0	$56,541	$0	$0	**$39,579**

The $39,579 after-tax withdrawal from the traditional 401(k) plan **must be added** to the **side account** Mr. Smith would have funded with the extra dollars he would have had available if he funded an income tax-deductible 401(k) plan instead of a cash value life insurance policy or traditional brokerage account after tax. From the side account, Mr. Smith could receive the following amounts <u>after tax</u> each year from ages 66-85:

- $16,533 in the 40% tax bracket
- $13,206 in the 30% tax bracket
- $7,031 in the 15% tax bracket

Totaling the numbers:

To compare numbers for the various wealth-building options for Mr. Smith, you really just need the total amount he can withdraw after tax from the traditional 401(k) plan and the after-tax side fund. From a regular 401(k) plan **plus** side account, Mr. Smith would receive, after tax, the following from ages 66-85:

- $50,458 in the 40% tax bracket
- $52,785 in the 30% tax bracket
- $55,091 in the 15% tax bracket

The previous numbers are what you need to keep in mind when I illustrate how much could have been taken out after tax from a cash value life insurance policy and a post-tax brokerage account.

2) 401(k) plan funding vs. life insurance

Again, this is one of the "**million-dollar questions**" in the finance-planning field. Is a tax-deferred 401(k) plan tax favorable or tax hostile? And how does funding a tax-deferred 401(k) plan (where money grows tax deferred but comes out and is fully taxable) compare to funding a cash value life insurance policy where it is funded after tax but then the cash in the policy **grows tax free** and **comes out tax free** in retirement.

You may have heard this question before:

Is it better to pay taxes on the "seed" or the "harvest"?

The seed is a contribution to a wealth-building plan, and the withdrawal of money from the plan is the harvest.

If you wonder what the following numbers will tell you, the answer is that it is better or even much better to pay taxes on the seed than the harvest.

Now that we have some 401(k) plan retirement numbers to work with, we can now compare them to repositioning money in a cash value life insurance policy.

When Mr. Smith repositions wealth in a life insurance policy, he will do so after tax.

Therefore, in this life insurance example, Mr. Smith will pay life insurance premiums of $15,000 a year from ages 45-65 and then borrow money "tax free" from his policy from ages 66-85. For illustration purposes, I will actually assume a little less than a 7% rate of return on the cash in the life insurance policy.

If Mr. Smith did, in fact, over-fund a low-expense, non-MEC equity indexed life insurance policy in the amount of $15,000 each year from ages 45-65, how much could he remove tax free from his life insurance policy income from ages 66-85?

$56,568 a year

Skeptical? How can that be? How can a cash value life insurance policy funded with after-tax dollars possibly outperform a traditional 401(k) plan?

If you read any of my other books, any of the hundreds of articles I've had published, or content on any of my web-sites, you should come to the conclusion very quickly that I do not have much tolerance for people who do not give full disclosure and for people who are not truthful when it comes to the math on financial topics.

No one is more of a skeptic than I am. Having said that, skepticism can easily be overcome when you look at the numbers for yourself. That's why I went out of my way to give you real-world math and the actual charts that go with the math.

The following spreadsheet comes right from an insurance company's software. It "is what it is" based on the assumptions (the main one being a 7% rate of return based on the S&P 500 index).

Age	Annual Premium	Cash Account Value	Death Benefit	"Tax-Free" Loans
45	$15,000	$0	$759,503	$0
50	$15,000	$65,289	$759,503	$0
55	$15,000	$169,098	$759,503	$0
60	$15,000	$321,249	$759,503	$0
65	$15,000	$546,163	$759,503	$0
70	$0	$446,393	$565,564	**$56,568**
75	$0	$328,067	$386,284	**$56,568**
80	$0	$191,117	$276,723	**$56,568**
85	$0	$30,145	$155,720	**$56,568**
90	$0	$183,162	$366,332	$0
95	$0	$506,151	$560,025	$0
100	$0	$1,118,146	$1,197,789	$0

Let me summarize the past few pages so I can bring this all together for those who are not quite following me.

Mr. Smith could invest in a traditional tax-deductible 401(k) plan, or he could reposition some of his money into a cash building life insurance policy to build his retirement nest egg.

To make a comparison to a traditional 401(k) plan, I had Mr. Smith tax deduct $15,000 into such a plan AND, depending on his income tax bracket, fund money into a side fund so he has the **same out-of-pocket costs** when funding the various wealth-building tools.

I then created three charts so you could review the outcome for yourself.

I created one chart for Mr. Smith in the 15% income tax bracket, one chart for the 30% income tax bracket, and one chart for the 40% income tax bracket. Remember that Mr. Smith's tax bracket doesn't matter when taking money out of a life insurance policy as there are no income taxes due (unlike when withdrawing money from a tax deferred 401(k) plan).

The following chart summaries the outcome.

	"After-Tax"
	Retirement Income
	Ages 66-85
Regular 401(k) (15% tax bracket)	$55,091
Regular 401(k) (30% tax bracket)	$52,785
Regular 401(k) (40% tax bracket)	$50,458
Cash Value Life Insurance	**$56,568**

I don't know about you, but I find the above chart and supporting math to be fascinating. Who knew that funding a cash value life insurance policy as an after-tax wealth-building tool could possibly work out better than funding the equivalent out–of–pocket amount of money into a tax-deferred 401(k) plan?

-Also keep in mind that Mr. Smith, in my example, also had a sizable initial death benefit ($759,000), which would pay income tax free upon death. The death benefit far exceeds the cash values in the 401(k) plans.

-Also keep in mind that Mr. Smith will have to pay a 10% penalty to remove money from his 401(k) plan before the age of 59.5 (with the exception of the annuitization option which most people will not want to use). There is no such penalty with a life insurance policy loan at any age.

-Also, keep in mind that Mr. Smith did not have to worry about the cash in his life insurance policy going backwards in a down market because of the annual locking feature in the life insurance policy (something that cannot be said of money in a traditional 401(k) plan that would have gone through the stock market crash of 2000-2002 and again in 2007-2009).

MORE REAL-WORLD MATH

Let's make the numbers a bit more real world. My previous numbers were <u>very conservative</u> and really made for example purposes only (since the assumed expenses were far too low to be real world).

Now let's assume that Mr. Smith's money in his traditional and regular 401(k) plan have the typical **1.2% mutual fund expense** and a .6% money management or "wrap" fee on the plans. How does that affect the numbers?

	"After-Tax"
	Retirement Income
	Ages 66-85
Regular 401(k) (15% tax bracket)	$43,761
Regular 401(k) (30% tax bracket)	$41,157
Regular 401(k) (40% tax bracket)	$38,676
Life Insurance Policy	**$56,568**

What's interesting is that the amount Mr. Smith can remove from his life insurance policy **does not change**, and the amount which can be withdrawn every year from the tax-deferred 401(k) plan are reduced quite a bit.

Why? Because I added on typical mutual fund annual expenses and the wrap fee typically associated with a company's 401(k) plan. Such expenses are not a variable in a cash value equity indexed life insurance policy.

I think this set of numbers is the most "real" world, but I did want to give you a few different looks at the numbers based on conservative expenses and typical expenses.

Interestingly, the cash value life policy returned **29% more income** if you are in the 15% income tax bracket, **37% better** if you are in the 30% bracket, and **46% better** if you are in the 40% income tax bracket.

Actually, the previous numbers have nothing to do with the real world. If you remember in the chapter on Traditional Wealth Building, the American public proved that when the S&P 500 returned **8.35%** from 1988-2008, the average investor returned than **1.87%** annually.

Let me throw one more little real-world twist in the equation. Do you remember the discussion in Chapter 3 about the **variable loan** option available in indexed equity life policies?

Most "experts" in the industry think that over time there will be a 2% positive spread between what the policies return every year (pegged to the S&P 500) and what the lending rates will be for loans on money borrowed from life insurance policies.

If I use just a 1% positive spread on the lending rate vs. the crediting rate in the life policy example, **how much more cash** could Mr. Smith remove tax free from his equity indexed life insurance policy?

Mr. Smith would be able to remove **$63,258** instead of **$56,568** from his policy from ages 66-85. Wow!

Just because I know your curiosity is getting the better of you, I figured I would give you the numbers for the 2% spread that "experts" think will happen. If the borrowing rate inside the life policy is 2% less than the assumed crediting rate for Mr. Smith, he could remove **$70,373** out of his policy from ages 66-85 instead of **$56,568.**

The following chart illustrates in a visual manner how much more wealth can be removed from cash value life insurance with variable loans (the tallest bars) and with wash loans (the middle set of bars) vs. how much could be removed after tax from a qualified retirement plan.

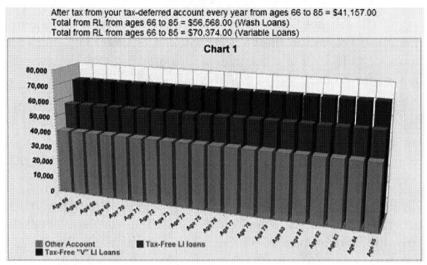

After tax from your tax-deferred account every year from ages 66 to 85 = $41,157.00
Total from RL from ages 66 to 85 = $56,568.00 (Wash Loans)
Total from RL from ages 66 to 85 = $70,374.00 (Variable Loans)

Very interesting, isn't it? What's interesting to me is that there are "what if" variables with an equity indexed cash value life insurance policy, which can really increase the amount borrowed. These variables are not available in a 401(k) plan.

Also, do NOT forget that the equity indexed life insurance policy has an annual locking feature for the gains; and the investment returns can never go negative due to down years in the stock market.

Let me illustrate one last example how much could be removed from a traditional 401(k) plan that <u>crashed 59%</u> **the year before Mr. Smith retired** vs. a EIUL policy that does not have such a problem.

I am going to assume that the market crashed just in that one year and then went back to a 7% gross rate of return for the withdrawal period. I am also using returns with a 1.2% mutual fund expense and a .6% wrap or money management fee in an attempt to create the most real-world numbers possible.

How much could be removed if Mr. Smith started and retired in the 30% income tax bracket? **$28,879**

With the EIUL policy, the built-up cash in the policy would not go backwards in the year when the stock market <u>crashed 59%</u>; and, therefore, the retirement income would hardly be affected (although it would be slightly less).

This protection afforded to people who use EUIL insurance is one of the main reasons many will choose to use EUIL to build wealth vs. stocks or mutual funds which provide **NO downside protection**.

3) Comparing post-tax investing in a brokerage account to funding cash value life insurance

In the previous material, I've shed some light on the real numbers that can be accumulated in a tax-deferred 401(k) plan and removed after tax in retirement. My guess is that most readers, before reading this book, were of the mind set that it is a very good idea to fund as much money as possible into a tax-deferred 401(k) plan.

If you are one such person after reading this book, you will have something to think about as an alternative (funding a tax-favorable and protective cash value life insurance after tax).

If you were/are of the opinion that funding a 401(k) plan is a good or the best way to build wealth in a tax-favorable manner, what are your thoughts about funding an **after-tax brokerage account** to build wealth?

Most people have some sort of brokerage account, whether the account is with a professional money manager or whether they day trade their own money online at places like E-Trade.

Obviously, you have to pay income taxes on your take-home income before you can invest your money in a brokerage account. Then when you invest in the stock market, you have to deal with <u>mutual fund expenses, money management fees, and dividend and capital gains taxes.</u>

In Chapter 1 on Traditional Wealth Building, I discussed, to my own amusement, how money grows in the stock market and how poorly the average investor did over the last 20 years. If you didn't read that chapter yet, please read it over. I think you'll find it fascinating reading.

Assuming that you've read how money grows in the real world in a brokerage account, let's get back to our Mr. Smith example and see how investing money in the stock market compares to positioning money for growth in a cash value life insurance policy.

Remember that I assumed Mr. Smith could find $15,000 to fund a cash value life insurance policy, which are after-tax investments.

On the next page is a condensed chart I created to show you how much money Mr. Smith could <u>remove from his brokerage account from ages 66-85.</u>

Remember he was 45 years old when he started funding his brokerage account for this example and funded it in the amount of $15,000 with after-tax dollars a year from ages 45-65. You'll also notice that I have different numbers depending on the assumed blended tax rate annually on the investments.

Blended annual tax rate	A	B	C	D	E
15%	$51,793	$46,874	$42,405	$38,346	
20%	$48,367	$44,020	$39,970	$36,442	
25%	$45,159	$41,333	$37,818	$34,592	
Average Investor Returns					**$23,040**

Just to remind you, from the EIUL policy, Mr. Smith could remove **$56,568** a year from ages 66-85 tax free with "wash loans."

The following are the variables used for A-E in the above chart, which as you can see changes the amount of money that can be taken out of Mr. Smith's brokerage account from ages 66-85:

A- NO mutual fund or money management fee

B- A .6% annual mutual fund expense (the industry average is 1.2%)

C-1.2% annual mutual fund expense

D-1.2% annual mutual fund expense AND .6% money management fee

E- NO mutual fund expense or money management fee. E is what the typical mutual fund investor earned with his/her investments invested from 1988-2008 without throwing in mutual fund expenses, money management fees, and taxes.

If you throw in a 1.2% mutual expense for E, the amount of money Mr. Smith could remove from a brokerage account drops down to **$18,062**.

What should first jump out at you is that the amount of money that can be removed from a post-tax brokerage account in any of the columns is **less** than what could be removed from almost all of the traditional 401(k) examples.

Therefore, if you were one of the many who believed that funding a traditional 401(k) plan was a better idea than paying tax on your money and investing post-tax in the stock market, **you were right**.

What should really jump out at you is that none of the columns have an annual withdrawal amount that are anywhere close to what Mr. Smith could remove from his life insurance policy via tax-free policy loans (**$56,568**) using conservative assumptions.

For many, this material will be counter-intuitive. Why? Because the vast majority of readers do not understand how financially viable an over-funded, low-expense, non-MEC cash-value life insurance policy can be when trying to grow wealth for retirement.

I could spend a lot more time explaining why specifically cash value life insurance outperforms traditional retirement plans and a post-tax brokerage account, but I believe for this type of book (which is not a technical certification course), simply showing you the charts so you can see it with your own eyes should be sufficient.

The bottom line with a comparison between funding an after-tax brokerage account vs. an EIUL policy is that there is no comparison given my real-world assumptions.

WHY HAVE MY CURRENT ADVISORS NOT DISCUSSED USING CASH VALUE LIFE INSURANCE AS A WEALTH-BUILDING TOOL AS AN ALTERNATIVE TO 401(K) PLANS OR POST-TAX BROKERAGE ACCOUNTS?

If you'll remember from the Foreword, I explained some of the problems in the financial services industry. Many Broker Dealers (the entity that most securities licensed advisors use to sell stocks and mutual funds through) **forbid** their licensed advisors from selling Equity Indexed Universal Life (EIUL) insurance policies.

Additionally, Broker Dealers do not like their advisors to use products that take money away from assets under management (which EIUL policies would certainly do if funded instead of 401(k) plans or post-tax brokerage accounts).

Couple the fact that most securities licensed advisors are not educated on EIUL policies with the fact that many Broker Dealers forbid or strongly discourage the use of such products, and it's no wonder that the vast majority of securities licensed advisors do not use EIULs or any kind of cash value life insurance as a protected and tax-favorable wealth-building tool.

This was the flaw in the financial planning area that cost millions of Americans billions of dollars when the stock market crashed in 2007-2009.

QUESTIONS TO PONDER

Question:

If you die before retirement, are you better off with a 401(k) plan or cash value life insurance?

Answer: Cash value life insurance - due to the fact that a large death benefit will be paid out income-tax free to the beneficiary and maybe estate-tax free.

Question: When do you have access to the money in a 401(k) plan or a cash value life insurance policy?

Answer: You have access to the cash in either; but with a tax-deferred 401(k) plan, there are negative tax consequences if the money is removed before age 59½ (although there is an exception for systematic payments paid prior to age 59½).

With a cash value life insurance policy, you have access to the cash immediately in two usable ways:

1) You can "surrender" the policy for the cash surrender value ("CSV"). This can work okay if you use a high early cash value indexed universal life insurance policy.

2) You can access the cash through tax-free loans anytime after you fund the policy (with no 10% penalty prior to age 59½).

For either 1) or 2), if you do not use a high cash value life insurance policy, the amount of cash you'll have access to will be limited in the first 10 years.

WHAT HAPPENS IF YOU ARE NOT HEALTHY OR HAVE MARGINAL HEALTH?

If you or your spouse (if you have one) are not healthy, using life insurance as a wealth-building tool becomes much more problematic. The costs of insurance annually inside the policy will significantly affect how much cash you will build and be able to borrow from in retirement from the policy.

As I try to do with all parts of this book, I like to put real-world numbers with every discussion.

Let's go back to our Mr. Smith. He was 45 years old and in good health. He funded a life insurance policy with $15,000 in annual premiums from 45-65. Then he could borrow **$56,568** a year from his life insurance policy income-tax free for 20 years (using the conservative assumptions). The assumed annual return was based on the S&P 500 index returning slightly less than 7%.

Let's now assume Mr. Smith has <u>average</u> (which in the insurance industry means below average) <u>health</u>. How will that affect the amount he can borrow from his policy?

He would only be able to borrow out **$5<u>2</u>,861** a year for 20 years instead of **$5<u>6</u>,586**. That's still quite a bit higher than what he would receive after tax from his traditional 401(k) plan and much more than funding an after-tax brokerage account in our previous example.

Let's now assume Mr. Smith is in <u>really bad health</u>. How does that affect the amount he can borrow from his life insurance policy?

If Mr. Smith was "table rated" E, he could expect to be able to borrow **$39,141** from his policy each year tax free from ages 66-85.

The table rating system at many insurance companies uses the alphabet. A is slightly rated, E is much worse, and P is just plain awful.

It is interesting to note that even if Mr. Smith is table E rated, the amount he can borrow from his policy is still higher than a few of the post-tax brokerage account outcomes.

Getting back to the real world, most people who read this book will be rated standard or better. Those who do not receive the top or close to the top table rating can use a spouse's life to help with the process and can even use a 2nd-to-die policy, which can also help lower the expenses.

WHAT IF A DIFFERENT COMPANY'S LIFE INSURANCE POLICY IS USED FOR THE ILLUSTRATION?

Great question.

For this book, I chose to use illustrations from the life insurance company I prefer to use with my favorite policy at that company (***Revolutionary Life***). There are many insurance companies that offer cash value life insurance policies.

As I indicated in the chapter in the book where I explained life insurance, my preference is to use equity indexed life insurance products because I believe over the long term they have the best chance for growth.

I also like the protective features which guard against losing money in the policy due to market forces.

If I used a different insurance company's indexed life policy, I could actually increase or decrease the numbers you'll read in this book. Life insurance is not the easiest wealth-building tool to understand; and at some point, you have to trust the advisor you are working with to put forth the best life insurance policy that will benefit you.

It means it is very important that readers find an advisor who knows "all" the useful cash-building policies and helps you choose one that is in your best interest, not that of the advisor.

Picking someone out of the phone book or from a radio or television ad is no way to find a financial planner who knows what he/she is doing.

If an advisor gave you a copy of this book to read, it's a good indication that he/she at the very least understands the concepts covered in this book (which puts him/her ahead of 95% of the rest of the advisors in the financial services field).

If you can't find an advisor you feel comfortable with, please feel free to e-mail (roccy@retiringwithoutrisk.com) or call me (269-216-9978); and I'd be happy to refer you to an advisor in your local area. I've trained thousands of advisors on the concepts covered in this book, and the chances of me having one in your local area are significant.

CHAPTER SUMMARY

I know that there are a lot of numbers and assumptions and tax brackets that are dealt with in this chapter. Many readers will have a bit of a headache after reading this chapter, and I certainly understand why.

Here are the bullet points that you should learn from this chapter:

-Do not put your blinders on and fund all of the money earmarked for retirement into a traditional 401(k) plan at work.

Once you understand the numbers, it will be in your best interest from a tax and protective point of view to allocate money to a properly designed cash value life insurance policy.

For those of you who understand how a low-expense, over-funded, non-MEC life insurance policy works as a retirement vehicle, you'll prefer to fund such a policy instead of funding your 401(k) plan. It sounds counter-intuitive, I know; but again, the numbers do not lie.

-It is clear that funding the proper cash value life insurance policy is a better idea for many than simply handing money over to a stockbroker or money manager.

The caveat to my previous statement is that the EIUL policies are never going to average returns in excess of 10%. I used examples in this book which are fairly conservative (investment returns of 7% (gross)).

If you have your money actively managed and earn in excess of 12% a year (gross), you will be better off after tax than funding a cash value life policy.

Of course, the caveat to the previous statement is when your money is actively traded in the stock market there are **no guarantees**; and if your money is in the market in a time span like what happened from 2000-2002 (<u>-46%</u>) or like what happened in 2007-2009 (<u>-59%</u>), you will wish you never had a dollar actively traded in the stock market (and that's the feeling of millions of Americans).

The bottom line is that there is no "right" answer or one perfect tool when it comes to building wealth. You've heard the saying, "Different strokes for different folks." It's that way with how you choose to build your wealth.

If you don't mind <u>risk</u>, you will not mind your money in the stock market, a 401(k) plan, or an after-tax brokerage account.

If you are **adverse to risk**, you will prefer the safety of the *appropriate* cash value life insurance policies, which have minimum guarantees and a large death benefit.

If you want to have your cake and eat it too, you will gravitate specifically to an equity indexed life insurance policy, which has tax-free accumulation, no money management fees, tax-free withdrawals, good growth pegged to one of the best measuring index, and principal protection from downturns in the market with a lock feature that never lets the money go backwards due to market declines.

Which option should you use to build your wealth?

I could not say for certain unless I looked at your individual situation; but hopefully after reading this book, you'll be armed with more information and knowledge to be better prepared to make decisions about which way is the best way to grow your wealth.

If you are over the age of 60 generally and, 65 specifically, you will enjoy the material in Chapters 6 and 7 where I explain the use of Fixed Indexed Annuities (FIAs) to grow your wealth. FIAs are not nearly as tax favorable as cash value life insurance; but they have features life insurance policies do not have, i.e., a **guaranteed rate of return of 7%** or more depending on the product (accumulation value) coupled with a **guaranteed income for life** you can never outlive.

Chapter 5
Understanding Annuities

If you've read Chapter 4, you might be of the opinion that the most protective and tax-favorable wealth-building tool at your disposal is a properly signed cash value life insurance policy.

That is, in fact, the case for many people; but there are no "secret" wealth-building tools and no "magic" concepts out there that are a good fit for everyone. As I stated, if you are over the age of 65, it is going to be difficult to make a cash value life insurance policy work as superior wealth-building tool.

Regardless of your age, one idea that has really taken hold in our society after the stock market crash of 2000-2002 (-46%) and again in 2007-2009 (-59% from highest point to lowest) is that of "**principal protection**."

Today, the American investor doesn't mind hearing about tools that will preserve principal. Prior to 2000 and, for some, prior to the end of 2007, the American investor thought that the stock market would forever provide returns in excess of 10% a year and, therefore, tools that protect principal were not needed (we now know those investors with such a mindset collectively lost billions of dollars in the two recent stock market crashes).

Generally speaking, when the American investor thinks of wealth-building concepts that preserve principal, they typically think of low-yielding tools like **certificates of deposits** (CDs), **money market accounts**, or potentially **"fixed" annuities**.

All three of the prior listed wealth-building tools guarantee your money will not go backwards, but the growth or return on each is typically very low (and CDs and money market accounts create annually taxable income).

The ironic thing is that, if the American investor had invested in any of these three tools and left the money in each for 20 years, they would have been better off or even significantly better off than what the average investor generated as returns (which if you'll remember was a **1.87%** annual average from 1998-2008).

What I will cover in the next chapter is a hybrid wealth-building tool called a **Fixed Indexed Annuity** (FIA). FIAs are unique wealth-building tools that in their "basic" form will be a good fit for many readers to grow wealth in a conservative manner.

By conservative manner, the numbers over time indicate that FIAs have returned approximately 2% more than traditional fixed tools such as CDs and money market accounts.

Two of the key features that make FIAs an attractive wealth-building tool are:

-FIAs guarantee your **money will NEVER go backwards** due to downturns in the stock market.

-FIAs **lock your gains every year;** and once locked in, they can never be lost due to a downturn in the stock market.

While the above sounds exciting, in the next chapter you'll read how a FIA can be used to **guarantee a certain rate of return** (accumulation value) such as **7%** coupled with a **guaranteed income for life** you can never outlive.

Also, some FIAs come with a FREE long-term care benefit (LTC) which is very exciting to many people who choose not to pay for traditional LTC insurance coverage.

In order to fully understand FIAs, it's important to have an education on annuities in general which is what I will cover in this chapter. You will not be an annuity expert after reading this chapter, but you will have a good base of knowledge that will help you whenever you decide to look at annuities as a wealth-accumulation/retirement tool.

TAX DEFERRED ANNUITIES

INTRODUCTION

In the past three decades, tax deferred annuities have emerged as a commonly used planning tool by financial advisors and estate planning attorneys as well as CPAs/accountants. As the financial services industry has undergone dramatic change, depository financial institutions, brokerage firms, and insurance companies have changed their product menus to appeal to a broader spectrum of the investing public.

As the country's population has increased in age, due to medical advancements that have increased longevity and the demographic bubble known as the "baby boomers," there has been an increased focus on retirement planning and **income planning** specifically.

As I stated in the Foreword, one of the problems facing the general public is the fact that most advisors do not have a full understanding of all the annuities available and how to use them to best help their clients.

Many securities licensed advisors know nothing or very little about FIAs, how they work, their living benefits, and guaranteed income riders.

The above stated fact is one of the main reasons I chose to write this book, i.e., to educate the American public on the power and protective nature of FIAs

WHAT IS AN ANNUITY?

An annuity is a contract between a buyer, or contract owner (typically an individual), and the issuer (typically an insurance company) whereby the contract owner agrees to pay the issuer an initial premium, or payment in a lump sum, or payments over a period of time, during which the issuer guarantees the owner a stated minimum rate of return or the opportunity to participate in the growth of an underlying group of assets in which the annuity premiums are invested. As with all contracts, there are numerous terms and conditions that influence the features and benefits that accrue to the owner.

The annuity contract is generally called a "Policy" because it is issued by an insurance company, and the owner is generally referred to as the "Policyholder." This terminology is used in general even though the annuity is technically not an "insurance policy" in the traditional sense; however, it may have some of the attributes of a life insurance policy, e.g., a death benefit. There are three general classifications of annuities: fixed, variable, and immediate. These will all be discussed.

There are generally three parties to an annuity: owner, annuitant, and beneficiary. The **owner** is the individual or individuals who own the cash benefits of the annuity. The owner is typically the only party who can redeem the annuity for its cash value, change beneficiaries, and make other changes allowed by the annuity contract. An annuity owner can be an individual, a trust, or a business entity.

The **annuitant** is generally the individual on whose life the death benefit is contingent. The annuitant may be, and oftentimes is, the same as the owner; but this is not required.

The **beneficiary** is the individual or entity who is named to receive the death benefit of the annuity.

The period of time that the annuity is growing in value, which may also be increased by additional premium payments into the annuity, is referred to as the **accumulation period**. The accumulation period may be indefinite such as the case with FIAs; or there may be a set limit, generally determined by the age of the owner or annuitant or a set period following the initial premium payment.

Once the end of the accumulation period is reached, the pay-out period of the annuity begins. During the pay-out period, the owner will receive a series of payments, or a lump sum, that is selected from a menu of options. Once the schedule of payments is completed, or upon death of the last named recipient if a "life only" payout is selected, the annuity ends and the contract, or policy, is terminated. A Single Premium Immediate Annuity ("SPIA," pronounced spee-uh) does not have an accumulation period and will be discussed later.

WHAT ARE THE COMMON CHARACTERISTICS OF ALL ANNUITIES?

TAX DEFRRAL

All tax qualified annuities, regardless of classification, offer income tax deferral of earnings until the earnings are withdrawn. This tax deferral feature of annuities has given rise to the saying that annuities enjoy "triple compounding:" interest on the principal, interest on the interest left in the annuity, and interest on the money that ordinarily would have been withdrawn to pay taxes. The only exception to this tax deferral exception is an annuity that is owned by an entity that is not an individual or in trust for an individual. Such entities are allowed to own annuities; however, there is no tax deferral generally available and an individual must be named as the annuitant.

WITHDRAWALS

Withdrawals from a tax-qualified annuity are currently subject to taxation on a last-in, first-out basis unless they are annuitized over a finite period of time or for life (meaning that withdrawal up to basis (the premiums paid) are subject to income taxes).

Taxation of an annuity is a non-issue when it is owned inside a qualified retirement plan or IRA due to the fact that all of the money coming out of either is fully income taxable.

ASSET PROTECTION

This "retirement purpose" of an annuity has also immunized them from creditors in many states. To learn if annuities in your state are protected from creditors, go to www.assetprotectionsociety.org; and you can find that information.

1035 EXCHANGES

One annuity may be exchanged for another annuity in accordance with the Internal Revenue Code Section 1035(e). Such 1035 exchanges do not trigger a taxable event and may be affected at any time regardless of the age of the owner or annuitant.

INVESTMENT PROTECTION

Because most non-variable annuities guarantee that your money will not go backwards, annuities provide investment/asset protection from downturns in the stock market.

Also, all annuities are also protected by the various State Guaranty Funds. These are reserve funds maintained by states to safeguard the cash value of policies, up to a certain limit, in the event an issuing insurance company is unable to meet its obligations under the contracts. To learn more about how much your state guarantees, e-mail info@retiringwithoutrisk.com.

PAYMENT OPTIONS

All annuities have options for payment during the payout phase. These range from a single lump sum payment to a periodic payment over the remaining life, or joint lives, of the annuitant or annuitants. In between, the owner may choose a period certain, usually no shorter than two years and no longer than thirty years. Also, the owner may select a payment for a period certain with a life option, meaning that, if the annuitant dies prior to the period certain (say 10 years), the payments would continue to the named beneficiary until the end of the stated period.

FIAs, which are the focus of the next chapter, do not have a set payout schedule. Typically what happens in retirement with a FIA is that an annuity owner will decide each year (or month or quarter) how much he/she would like to withdraw from the annuity (without limitation after the surrender charge period is over). You might think of the ability to withdraw similar to taking money out of a savings account when needed.

As you will read in the next chapter, if you buy a FIA with a guaranteed income for life, there will be a payment schedule guaranteed by the insurance company; but that will not preclude an owner from still having access in full to the remaining account balance.

DEATH BENEFITS

Death benefits are also a common feature of all annuities. Some annuities impose the surrender penalties, if still in force, at death whereas others do not. FIAs typically have no surrender charges applied to the death benefit no matter when the annuitant dies.

It should be noted that death benefits from an annuity contract do not pass income and estate tax free like life insurance death proceeds can.

SURRENDER CHARGES

Surrender charges for early surrender are almost universal for annuities. These charges are imposed for a stated period of time, generally from one to twenty years depending on the annuity. These charges are deducted from the cash amounts of the policy prior to being paid to the policyholder.

Surrender charges are clearly stated in the contract and characteristically decline each year after the first and disappear at the end of the stated period. For example, a "typical" annuity might have ten years of surrender charges beginning at 10% in year 1 and stepping down 1% per year and completely disappearing at the end of 10 years.

Surrender charges only come into play if an owner decided to literally surrender (cash in) the annuity.

Surrender charges are very misunderstood by many financial commentators and certainly by many state insurance departments. There has been a movement among regulators to limit the length of the surrender-charge period in annuities. It sounds consumer friendly, but it's not. Limiting insurance companies from offering products with longer surrender charges limits the variety of products offered in the marketplace, and that is never good for the consumer.

What regulators do not understand is that the longer the surrender period of the annuity the better the terms (typically).

It is rare for me to say a product is bad or evil. That's what has happened to a fewer longer surrender charge annuities. Regulators are equating a long surrender charge with a "bad" or not very "consumer friendly" product.

In my opinion, the problem is not a product with a long surrender charge; it's the use of the product that's the problem. Let me ask you few simple questions that I think will illustrate my point.

"Should a 75-year old person be sold an annuity with a 15-year surrender charge"? The answer is probably not because, in order to have access to all the cash, he/she would have to wait 15 years.

"Should a 60 year old be sold an annuity with a 15-year surrender charge"? The answer is maybe. It's always a facts and circumstances question.

What if the 15-year surrender charge annuity had much better terms than a 5-year surrender charge annuity and the 60 year old didn't need access to "all" the money in the annuity for years to come? What should the prospective buyer do?

Again, it depends; but this example client may choose to buy a 5-year surrender charge annuity with X amount of money, a 10-year surrender charge annuity with X amount of the money, and a 15-year surrender charge annuity with X amount of the money. This is called laddering and is something that will make sense for many people looking to buy annuities.

My point with this detailed discussion about surrender charges is that annuities with longer surrender periods typically have better terms; and with "proper" planning, you should be able to find annuities that fit with your long-term plan and give you the best terms for financial success.

FREE WITHDRAWALS

Most FIAs specifically have a 10% free withdrawal option every year. How does it work? No matter what the surrender charge or period is, you can always remove 10% of your account balance from the annuity every year without penalty. Some companies also allow for a 20% withdrawal once during the contract period.

Therefore, even if you had a 15-year surrender charge annuity, you could take 10% of the account balance out every year without a penalty.

Many annuities also have free withdrawal provisions of all or some of the annuity funds if the owner and/or annuitant are confined to a nursing home. Another free withdrawal rider covers the diagnosis of terminal illness of the owner and/or annuitant.

PENALTIES

In addition to early surrender charges that are imposed by the issuer, the Internal Revenue Service ("IRS") assesses a 10% penalty tax on earnings that are withdrawn if the owner is under age 59½ at the time of the withdrawal. There are numerous exceptions to the rule, e.g., disability, if taken in substantially equal payments over the remaining life of the owner, if the payments are from a Single Premium Immediate Annuity (SPIA).

BONUS PREMIUMS

In recent years, the "bonus premium" or "bonus interest rate" has been a common feature of annuities.

Bonuses are typically paid in the same year as the premium paid and are based on the initial premium payment (although not always). The size of these up-front bonuses range from as low as 1% percent to as high as 25%.

Up-front bonus annuities have proven to be very powerful from a marketing perspective for insurance companies. This makes sense if you think about it. The sales pitch goes something like this: "Would you like me to show you a wealth-building tool where the day you fund it your account balance is 10% higher than what you contributed? Therefore, if you allocate $100,000 to this wealth-building tool, from day one, your account balance for growth purposes is $110,000."

There is nothing wrong per se with bonus annuities. Just make sure you understand what the insurance company is doing to recoup its bonus money. It might be that the surrender charge without the bonus would have been 5 years and with the bonus it's 10 years.

You do need to check the fine print when you buy an annuity with a bonus. With some companies, the bonuses are lost if the owner dies prior to the end of the surrender period or if the owner takes the funds in a lump sum, i.e., does not annuitize for a certain time period at the end of the surrender period.

ANNUITIZATION

Annuitization is sometimes a dirty word when it comes to annuities. When you "annuitize" an annuity, you are telling the insurance company to take the money you have in the annuity and to guarantee a payout for a period of time (usually the remaining life of the annuitant). When you annuitize the annuity, you are trading the ability to withdraw cash from the annuity for the guaranteed payout. Therefore, if you had a crisis in your life that you needed cash to fix or mitigate it, if you annuitize your annuity, you will no longer have an ability to take a cash withdrawal; and you are stuck with the period annuitized payment.

To many, a guaranteed payment sounds appealing. However, with the FIA guaranteed income riders you'll read about in the next chapter that DO NOT require you to annuitize the annuity to receive an income stream for life, the need to annuitize an annuity has decreased dramatically.

TAXATION OF ANNUITIZED PAYMENTS

The taxation of payments in annuitization from non-qualified funds (those not in a qualified retirement plan such as IRA, 401(k), etc.) is determined by the "exclusion ratio." The exclusion ratio is computed by dividing the amount of the initial premium by the sum of the payment to be received (determined by the mortality tables for life-only pay-out options). The exclusion ratio, which will always be less than 100%, is then multiplied by the periodic payment to determine the amount of the payment that is excluded from taxation. The amount that is not taxed, i.e., excluded, is classified as return of principal. Obviously, if the annuity being annuitized contained qualified funds, then all the income would generally be taxable if the original contributions were made in before-tax dollars.

SALES LOADS

I've already discussed "surrender charges" in an earlier section that typically apply to fixed annuities.

Variable annuities (VA), on the other hand, can have up-front sales charges (loads) as well as on-going charges for management and other expenses associated with overseeing the portfolio of underlying assets (including back-end sales loads). The sales and on-going charges of VAs will be listed in the prospectus and should be reviewed carefully before purchasing.

The average ongoing expenses in a VA are <u>2.2%-2.7%</u> per year. This is a heavy price to pay especially when there is NO principal protection in the product (unless you add riders that also come with an additional cost).

WHAT ARE THE DIFFERENT CLASSIFICATIONS OF ANNUITIES?

VARIABLE ANNUITIES (VAs)

The broadest classification of annuities is between fixed and variable. VAs are "securities" because, as the name implies, their value can vary, positive and negative, from the original amount of premium paid. VAs are oftentimes referred to as "mutual funds inside an insurance wrapper" because, while the earnings are tax-deferred, the underlying assets are the same or similar to those associated with mutual funds, i.e., stocks, bonds, market indexes, and general securities. Additionally, the fee structure for variable annuities is similar to mutual funds since they can include an up-front sales charge as well as on-going administrative and money management fees. In the absence of riders, the variable annuity generally does not carry any guarantees in regard to minimum earnings, death benefits, or lifetime income amounts.

Like mutual funds, variable annuities carry the <u>risk of loss</u> unless the buyer chooses one or more of the riders that prevent or reduce loss. These riders are generally minimum guaranteed death benefits, minimum guaranteed income benefits, and guaranteed withdrawal benefits.

The guaranteed minimum death benefit warrants that generally the value of the annuity upon the death of the owner and/or annuitant will be the highest year-end value reached by the annuity during the holding period.

If you add up all the fees on the various "riders" on VAs, they can add an additional **3.20%** on top of the average other typical annual fees of **2.2%-2.7%** per year. To say that VAs are very expensive would be an understatement. However, if the annual investment return is high enough in a VA, the expenses can be justified. (Everyone loves VAs in bull stock market runs and wishes they'd never heard of them when the market crashes).

Also, if you'll recall, the average mutual fund investor from 1988-2008 earned a return of **1.87%**. Since VAs typically mirror the returns in mutual funds (but done inside a tax-free wrapper as far as the annual growth is concerned), VAs over that time frame may have had a negative average rate of return (and remember that the S&P 500 index from 1988-2008 averaged **8.35%**).

FIXED ANNUITIES

The fixed annuity's prime characteristic is that it guarantees some minimum earning rate if held for the contractual term, generally defined as the length of the surrender penalty period.

The minimum guaranteed growth is most often stated as some base interest rate, e.g., 2.5%, (a) during the period from the initial premium payment until the end of the penalty, and (b) during the total time that the owner holds the annuity in the accumulation phase. It is important to note that some issuers state their guaranteed minimum as a given rate on a percent of the initial premium, e.g., 3% on 90% of the initial premium. It is tempting to conclude that this arrangement would yield a 2.7% minimum guarantee, but doing the math will show a much lower minimum guarantee.

As I will explain in the next chapter, the index-linked fixed annuity has many of the characteristics of a variable annuity with respect to the earnings opportunity; but it still carries some minimum guaranteed earnings rate if held to term. The fixed annuity has sometimes been characterized as offering a "guaranteed return" whereas the variable annuity offers a "guaranteed opportunity" to realize a return.

SINGLE PREMIUM IMMEDIATE ANNUITY

A narrower classification identifies annuities according to function of how they are funded. For example, the Single Premium Immediate Annuity ("SPIA") involves the payment of a single premium followed no later than one year with a stream of income payment. SPIAs can be either fixed or variable and should not be confused with an annuity that is in the payout phase. While both involve a stream of income payments, the SPIA has no accumulation phase.

SINGLE PREMIUM DEFERRED ANNUITY

Annuities, both fixed and variable, may be "single premium" or "flexible premium." The former is referred to as SPDA (single premium deferred annuity) and the contract allows only one initial premium whereas the FPDA (flexible premium deferred annuity) allows additional premiums after the initial premium. These additional premiums usually must be at least a certain minimum amount and may be limited to one or more years following the initial premium.

TAX SHELTER ANNUITIES

A special class of annuities is the Tax Shelter Annuities ("TSA") and is governed by Section 403(b), 457 and others of the Internal Revenue Code. TSAs can be fixed or variable. Generally, TSAs are available to the employees of public institutions (school teachers and policemen, as well as those of non-profit organizations), certain hospitals, and the clergy. Premiums are paid in before tax dollars, making all withdrawals subject to ordinary taxation. The TSA generally can be opened for a very small amount, $100; and subsequent premiums may also be small. Premium payments are routinely made through payroll deductions. The contribution and withdrawal rules vary widely according to the individual circumstances of the owner.

INDEXED LINKED FIXED ANNUITIES ("FIA")

The index linked fixed annuity is commonly referred to as a Fixed Indexed Annuity (FIA). When this annuity was introduced, it was linked to an equity index only and thus the reason for the name.

The next chapter of this book will fully explain how FIAs work and their benefits, and so I will not take up time to discuss FIAs in this chapter.

TWO-TIER ANNUITIES (non-walk away)

No discussion of annuities would be complete without mentioning the concept of a "two-tier" annuity. This brand of annuity can come in any form.

A two-tier (also known as a non-walk away) annuity is given its name because of the seemly forced manner the insurance company makes you take your income.

Tier one is the accumulation phase. This may include a bonus when the annuity was purchased and a specific crediting rate during the accumulation phase.

Tier two is the payout phase. In the payout phase, if you want to partake of all of the benefits of the bonus and/or specified crediting rate during the accumulation phase, the income from the annuity MUST be taken out per the requirements of the annuity contract.

So what? The so what comes into play when an annuity owner didn't really understand the terms of the payout phase and then learns that the payout MUST be over a certain number of years (like 10 years).

Therefore, if the annuity owner has a financial crisis or a need for lump sum cash from the annuity, while he/she could request it, the punishment levied upon the account balance prior to distribution can be significant (the loss of bonus or a reduced crediting rate over the accumulation phase which will significantly lower the available lump sum amount available for distribution).

Also, one of the not-so-talked-about issues with this type of annuity is that in the income phase (when the annuity owner is forced to take money out of the annuity over a period of time), there is no guarantee on what the rate of return on the account balance will be over this time period.

For example, the annuity may have returned 6% during the accumulation phase. However, in the payout phase, the effective return on the account balance may only be 2-3%. Generally speaking, most non-walk away annuities do not specify the rate of return the annuity will be credited within the payout phase. I'm certain that the rate will be a percentage that ensures that the insurance company makes a nice profit on the annuity (meaning, if the company didn't price it right when it was sold, it will make up for it by punishing the annuity owner in the payout phase).

As you can guess, there has been massive litigation over these products when the annuity owner who didn't really understand that he/she would lose the 20% bonus, for example, if he/she doesn't take the payout over 10+ years.

While the product itself is not evil, how the product has been sold in the past leaves quite a bit to be desired. I personally have very little use for these products; and FYI, many of them have been pulled from the market.

USING ANNUITIES INSIDE QUALIFIED RETIREMENT PLANS OR IRAS

One issue I have not discussed in any detailed manner but wanted to touch on before moving to the next chapter is the argument against using annuities inside of qualified plans (401(k)) or IRAs.

Many CPAs for some reason caution clients to watch out for advisors selling tax-deferred annuities inside tax-deferred vehicles like 401(k) plans or IRAs. The argument is that the advisor is looking to make a quick commission when there is no benefit to using a tax-deferred vehicle inside a tax-deferred vehicle.

What the CPAs and others making this argument do not understand is that the reason the annuity is being purchased is for its protective features (money never goes backwards), for a guaranteed rate of return (accumulation value) coupled with an income for life you can never outlive, and for living benefits such as a FREE LTC benefit.

When lecturing on the proper use of annuities, I typically recommend that people buy them inside qualified retirement plans or IRAs because the growth on the annuity will all be income taxable regardless of whether it is coming out of an annuity or not.

If you happen to run into a CPA or other advisor who makes this argument, do him/her a favor and buy him a copy of my book. If you tell me you are giving it to a CPA for this reason, call me; and I'll sell you the book at my cost.

Finally, if you have vested money in a qualified retirement plan at work and if the plan does not allow for the purchase of annuities, there is a process to roll the money out of the plan into an IRA while still working. Doing so would then allow you to choose your own wealth-building tools with that money which could be the use of an annuity.

SUMMARY OF THE BASICS OF ANNUITIES

Annuities come in many varieties, classifications, and versions; but they all have in common the feature of tax deferral. Annuities have a place in the financial plans for a large percentage of the individuals who are saving for retirement or who are already in retirement and who **cannot afford to take the risk of losing some or all of their retirement nest egg**.

While annuities are not for everyone, they are appropriate for conservative savers who cannot afford or choose not to afford stock market risk.

Finally, Fixed Indexed Annuities, as you will read the next chapter, are the only wealth-building tool that can offer all the following benefits:

-100% principal protection from downside risk
-Zero up-front sales fees
-The opportunity to earn a competitive rate of return (and even a guaranteed rate of return (accumulation value), and
-A guaranteed lifetime income that cannot be outlived

Chapter 6
Building Wealth with
Fixed Indexed Annuities (FIAs)

For readers who lost <u>40-50-60%</u> when the stock market crashed in 2007-2009, this will be one of the most exciting chapters of any book you'll ever read.

In this chapter, I will go over in detail Fixed Indexed Annuities (FIAs) and why you should be using them as one of your wealth-building tools.

Why FIAs? Because they can have the following characteristics:

-**100% principal protection** (your money will never go backwards due to negative returns in the stock market).

-**Positive gains** in a stock index are **locked in every year** (minus dividends).

-A **guaranteed rate of return** (accumulation value) between **4%-8%** depending on the product.

-A **guaranteed income for life** you can never outlive (without having to annuitize).

-A **free long-term care benefit**

Does a wealth-building tool with the above-mentioned characteristics interest you?

I'd be shocked if it didn't.

-What's sadly ironic as you read in the Foreword of this book is that the vast majority of securities licensed advisors (those who primarily sell stocks and mutual funds to make a living) either know nothing or very little about FIAs.

-What's worse is that many Broker Dealers who securities licensed advisors sell their stock and mutual funds through <u>forbid the advisors from selling</u> or <u>discussing</u> FIAs with clients.

-What's worse is that most of these same advisors who are forbidden from selling FIAs <u>do NOT disclose</u> that to the clients or potential clients they are supposedly helping build wealth.

With proper asset allocation using FIAs as a wealth-building tool, the pain of the recent stock market crash could have been significantly mitigated. Unfortunately, the vast majority of advisors giving stock and mutual fund advice do not use FIAs to help their clients; and, therefore, the stock market crash took a heavy toll on most American investors.

Enough with my commentary about what's wrong with the financial services industry. Let me move on to discuss the very powerful and protective FIA.

WHAT IS A FIXED INDEXED ANNUITY?

As the name indicates, a "fixed" indexed annuity is classified as a "fixed" annuity. As such, the product must be equipped with guarantees that non-fixed/variable annuities do not.

Generally speaking, most advisors explain that a FIA has a **guaranteed return of zero** in any given year. Therefore, when the stock market goes negative, the returns in the FIA do not; and the annuity owner is credited with a zero rate of return in negative years.

There are actual minimal contractual guarantees in a FIA (although understanding them can be a bit difficult). The following is a typical contractual guarantee from a FIA contract:

This FIA provides a guaranteed minimum value to your annuity called the Policy Value. The Death Benefit, the Annuitization Value, and the Cash Value can never be less than the Policy Value. The calculation of the Policy Value is independent of the calculation of the Accumulation Value for the first 10 Policy Years. The Policy Value is an accumulation of 87.5% of the premium at an annual rate of at least 2.45% for the first six Policy Years and at least 1% thereafter.

The above is probably clear as mud. The bottom line with the guarantee is that, once funded, the money will **never go backwards** due to negative returns in the stock market. The guarantee, which is typically over a multi-year period, usually doesn't come into play due to the fact that FIAs usually yield better returns than the minimal guarantees; and, therefore, a FIA usually will have 0% credited in years when the measuring index goes negative.

What people are most interested in is what does the word "**indexed**" stand for and why is that used in the name of a "fixed" product?

The indexed part of the name alludes to the fact that the **gains in a FIA track a particular stock index** (minus dividends). The preferred stock index that has been used since the inception of FIAs over ten years ago is the Standard and Poor's 500 stock index (although other stock indexes are now available such as the DJIA, Wilshire 2000, and NASDAQ).

The S&P 500 index is widely regarded as one of the best single gauge of the U.S. equities market and represents a sample of 500 public companies in the U.S. economy.

As you previously read, even after the stock market crash of 2007-2009 where the S&P 500 index went down **38%** in 2008 alone, the index has still averaged **8.35%** from 1988-2008. Unfortunately, the "average" mutual fund investor over this same time frame only averaged a return of **1.83%**.

IF YOU ONLY KNEW!

If you only knew the stock market was going to crash in 2000-2002 and again in 2007-2009, wouldn't you have taken your money out of the market? Of course, we all would have.

The following picture illustrates in general how a FIA works in both positive and negative years in the stock market. You'll notice that, in negative years, the account value (represented by the dark line that looks like a ladder) does not decrease; it flatlines.

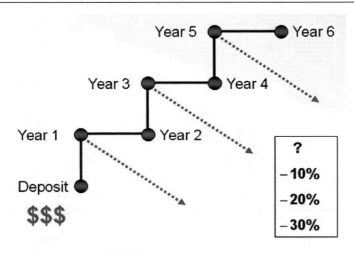

ZERO IS YOUR HERO

A good saying when the market goes negative is that "zero is the hero." It's a saying that people who had FIAs during the 2000-2002 and 2007-2009 stock market crashes started to use.

Instead of going over to your neighbor's house and bragging about how well your stocks did in a bull market (which many people have a tendency to do), you would go over there and brag about how you earned ZERO. It's crazy; but in the volatile environment we are in, when the stock market goes negative (or very negative) in a short period of time, zero sure is your hero.

Looks look at an example of zero being your hero over a five-year period with returns of 14.71%, -22%, -11%, -9%, and 21% where the starting account value is $100,000.

	$100,000	$100,000
	Invested in S&P	**Invested in FIA**
Year	**A**	**B**
1	$114,710	$112,000
2	$89,370.56	$112,000
3	$78,753.34	$112,000
4	$71,586.78	$112,000
5	$86,648.64	$122,080

As you can see, when the stock market goes backwards, so does the account balance invested in the S&P 500 stock index. However, in those same negative years, the FIA flatlined and held its highest value which came at end of year one.

Also, you'll notice that, in the first positive year, the account value in the S&P 500 index was higher than the FIA account balance. That's because most FIAs have caps on the upside growth (as you will read); and in this particular example, the cap in year one was 12%.

In the following pages, you will learn in detail how FIAs work to grow and protect your wealth. The following material is fairly detailed, but I wanted to put it in the book for those readers who really like to know details.

If you are not too interested in the mechanics of how FIAs work, you can skip over some of the following material and jump ahead to the section in this chapter titled, "Does Buy and Hold Work in a Volatile Stock Market?"

FIAs are not the perfect wealth-building tool. However, based on their protective design, it is easy for millions of Americans to justify having some portion of their retirement money allocated to these products.

Let me ask you again, "**If you only knew**," wouldn't you have had **some or even a significant amount of your money** in a principally guaranteed FIA over the last ten years?

DOES THE INSURANCE COMPANY REALLY INVEST YOUR MONEY IN THE S&P 500 STOCK INDEX?

No. As I explained in an earlier chapter, when I first looked at FIAs ten years ago, I thought that's exactly what the insurance companies did with the premium dollars (i.e., invest it in the actual stock index which has NO downside protection). I figured this was a risky thing for an insurance company do to, but it seemed like insurance companies owned half the investments in this world and I figured they could afford to take that risk.

Although the gains are linked to the S&P 500 stock index (minus dividends), the premium dollars paid by insureds are not actually invested in the S&P 500 index (which would be very risky).

The following is a simple explanation of how an insurance company can guarantee that money will not go backwards in a FIA and allow gains at market rates (up to a cap) with very little risk.

1) The insurance company receives an annuity owner's premium payment and invests the money in **income-producing bonds**.

2) Income from the bonds is then used to **purchase options** on the S&P 500 stock index. (For an example of how option purchases are used by insurance companies to hedge risk and increase returns, turn back to Chapter 3).

The return of the S&P 500 options drives the returns in the FIA. With higher bond income, the insurance company can buy more options that can generate better returns and higher caps in the FIA.

It is because of the above variables that the "**caps**" in the products (explained in an upcoming section) will have slight fluctuations.

What's important to understand is that, even if the S&P 500 stock index goes down 50%+ (like it did in a stretch of time between 2007-2009), the insurance company is not overly affected when it comes to the FIA portfolio. Remember, the premium dollars are in income-producing bonds, not the actual index. Therefore, after a year when the stock market declines significantly, the bond portfolio is still there and will still generate an income that can be used to buy options on the stock index to drive the following year's return in the FIA.

Logically speaking, the decline in the stock market as a whole may have an effect on the amount of income from the bonds and that would affect the option purchase (which could cause a reduction in caps in the product).

The exact link between the earning potential of the FIA and the index to which it is linked can vary widely among issuers and even annuities issued by the same insurance company. The method used to compute the earnings of the FIA is referred to as the "crediting method" and each method has its own unique set of terms and conditions. In fact, at the time this book is being published, there are over fifty different crediting methods in use and the number continues to expand.

CASH ACCOUNT VALUE (CAV) VS. CASH SURRENDER VALUE (CSV)

FIAs, like cash value life insurance, have a CAV and a CSV. The CAV is the money inside your FIA that is actually growing. The CSV is what you would receive if you said to the insurance company that you no longer wanted the annuity and would like your money back.

The CAV and the CSV are typically the same account value after the surrender charge period has expired.

When growth is credited to your FIA, it is credited based on your CAV. This is important to understand especially when dealing with annuity bonuses (discussed in an upcoming section).

For example: Assume you paid a $100,000 premium into a FIA that has a 10% first-year surrender charge.

If the S&P 500 index returns 5% in year one, that 5% is credited based on your CAV not your CSV.

Therefore, at the beginning of **year two**, the CAV would be $105,000; and the surrender charge base may, for example purposes, drop from 10% down to 9%.

If you surrendered your FIA for cash in year two, you would receive 91% of $105,000.

CREDITING METHODS

One of the most popular crediting methods to calculate the gain in a FIA is called the **annual point-to-point** method.

It works as follows: At the time of the initial FIA premium, the level of the S&P 500 index is recorded as the starting point and is then compared to the level of the index at the first anniversary date 12 months later. The difference in value (if positive) is used to determine the amount of earnings paid into the annuity for the first year.

For example: If the S&P 500 index has a value of **1,000** when a FIA is funded on January 15th and on January 15th the following year the value is **1,050**, the FIA would be credited with growth of 5% (1,000/1,050 = a 5% return).

For Example: If the S&P 500 index has a value of **1,000** when the FIA is funded on January 15th and on January 15th the following year the value is **950**, the FIA would be credited with growth of 0% because FIAs do not partake in the downside of the market.

Additionally, the following year, if the S&P 500 index goes positive by 5%, the FIA would be credited with a gain starting with the already higher account balance vs. a brokerage account that would go down with the market in year two and where any following upturn in the market would then be based on a lower account value (see the next chart for an example).

The following example will illustrate how important it is to not go backwards when the stock market goes negative and to lock in gains when the market moves in a positive direction.

	Account Balance FIA	Account Balance Brokerage Account
Start Balance	$100,000	$100,000
End of year 1 (**+5%**)	$105,000	$105,000
End of year 2 (-5%)	$105,000	$99,750
End of year 3 (**+5%**)	**$110,250**	**$104,740***

*This does not take into account the typical mutual fund fees applied to a brokerage account. If a 1.2% mutual fund expense is levied upon the brokerage account, the balance at the end of year three would be **$101,060**.

CAPS

From what you've read so far you may be saying to yourself that FIAs are the greatest thing you've ever heard about. No losses, locking in of gains annually, etc.

As we all know, rarely is there a free lunch in this world (FIAs are no different). FIAs have "caps" on the amount of growth in the product.

Most of the FIAs in the marketplace have caps that literally cap the gains of the annuity over a specified time frame.

With an annual point-to-point FIA, the annual cap typically would range from 5%-12+% depending on certain variables.

What variables? 1) How much income is produced from the bonds the insurance company purchases with your premium and 2) the cost of the options on the measuring index.

If the bond income is high and/or the option costs are low, the insurance company is then in a position to raise the caps on its products. In an environment where bond income falls and option costs increase, the insurance companies typically will be forced to lower the caps to keep profitability.

As stated, the caps with most FIAs can change periodically. For an annual point-to-point annuity, the cap could change annually. For example, back in 1999, the annual caps on some FIAs were as high as 12%. When the market tanked the following three years, the caps with some companies went down as low as 4% (although most quality companies still kept their caps at 6.5% or higher).

With all FIAs, there is a contractual agreement that the company will not go below a certain cap number (like no lower than 3% annually on an annual point-to-point product).

Those "in the know" in the financial services/insurance industry know that certain companies like to play games with their caps. Those are companies consumers should stay away from.

What games are played? Some companies have a history of offering high caps in the year the FIA is issued to entice consumers to buy their products and then lower the caps significantly the next year (whether the economic environment dictates lowering the cap or not).

MONTHLY CAPS

Some products have what are known as monthly caps. Instead of determining the return on an annual basis, the FIA is designed to calculate the returns on a monthly basis with a monthly cap.

The sales pitch is fairly enticing as compared to a less exciting annual point-to-point product. Let's assume the monthly cap is 3%. An advisor looking to entice a client to use a monthly point-to-point product would illustrate to a client that 12 months times the cap of 3% equals a "potential" return of 36% (which is much higher than what could be credited in an annual point-to-point that at its highest point may have a cap reaching 12%).

It sounds great doesn't it? Shouldn't we all buy monthly crediting FIAs?

Let's look at the downside. While there is a cap on the returns, there is **no cap on the losses** in each month. Let me illustrate how a monthly point-to-point FIA can credit a zero rate of return when over a 12-month period the index actually had a positive return.

Example: Assume that the measuring stock index started with a balance of **1,000**. In the next chart, you will see the monthly returns. You'll also notice that the ending account balance of the S&P 500 index is **1,082**. Therefore, in an annual point-to-point FIA, the return would have been +8% (assuming the annuity had a cap rate of 8% or more).

Month	Start of Month Balance	Gain or Loss	Month End Index Value	Index Returns
1	**1,000**	60	1,060	6%
2	1,060	0	1,060	0%
3	1,060	64	1,124	6%
4	1,124	-112	1,011	-10%
5	1,011	71	1,082	7%
6	1,082	-32	1,050	-3%
7	1,050	0	1,050	0%
8	1,050	63	1,113	6%
9	1,113	56	1,168	5%
10	1,168	-58	1,110	-5%
11	1,110	67	1,176	6%
12	1,176	-94	**1,082**	-8%

Let's look at the following chart using the same numbers as the above chart except I will illustrate the numbers using a <u>monthly</u> 3% cap FIA. You'll notice that I substituted 3% as the maximum gain in any month. When you use a monthly cap product where you have significant down months, you can actually have a negative return in a year when the measuring index is positive.

Month	Start of Month Balance	Gain or Loss	Month End Index Value	Index Returns
1	**1,000**	30	1,030	3%
2	1,030	0	1,030	0%
3	1,030	31	1,061	3%
4	1,061	-106	955	-10%
5	955	29	983	3%
6	983	-30	954	-3%
7	954	0	954	0%
8	954	29	983	3%
9	983	29	1,012	3%
10	1,012	-51	961	-5%
11	961	29	990	3%
12	990	-79	**911**	-8%

In the previous chart, the return for the year is negative; and, therefore, the amount credited in a monthly cap product for this example year would be 0% (at a time when the annual point-to-point product had an 8% positive return).

I don't want to give monthly caps products a bad stigma, so let me show you the positive side of using a monthly cap product in the following chart.

Month	Start of Month Balance	Gain or Loss	Month End Index Value	Index Returns
1	**1,000**	30	1,030	3%
2	1,030	0	1,030	0%
3	1,030	31	1,061	3%
4	1,061	0	1,061	0%
5	1,061	32	1,093	3%
6	1,093	0	1,093	0%
7	1,093	33	1,126	3%
8	1,126	34	1,159	3%
9	1,159	35	1,194	3%
10	1,194	-60	1,134	-5%
11	1,134	34	1,168	3%
12	1,168	-47	**1,122**	-4%

Using the previous chart, the return of the monthly cap product would be approximately 11.2%. The annual cap product would have reached its cap with a return of 8% (assuming a 8% cap).

The bottom line with monthly cap products is that they perform well when the measuring index is steadily increasing. If that happens, a monthly cap product will significantly outperform an annual point-to-point product.

However, if things are volatile, a monthly cap product as you've seen can actually have a negative return in a year when the measuring index is positive.

MONTHLY AVERAGING

I'm not going to spend much time explaining how a monthly average crediting method works. Why? Because over nearly every time frame in our stock market's history, returns in averaging products have lagged the point-to-point crediting method.

The return in a monthly average FIA is based on the total index performance from each month in the year divided by the total number of months or 12. The index closing value is recorded on the same day of each month after the policy is issued and then averaged out at the end of the year. The monthly average gain is then added to the annuity policy at the end of the year and locked in.

Advocates for the monthly average return method point out that the use of an averaging method reduces the volatility and can, therefore, increase the returns. This is true; but as I stated earlier, if you back test a monthly average product, the returns have significantly lagged the returns of an annual point-to-point method.

Without getting too complicated, when insurance companies issue a monthly averaging product, the costs on the options are significantly less—so much so that many monthly average products have NO CAP. No cap sounds much better than an annual cap of 6.5-12%; but again, after doing my research, I've not found a monthly averaging product (even with no cap) that would have consistently earned better returns than an annual point-to-point FIA.

OTHER CREDITING METHODS

There are several other crediting methods in the FIA marketplace. I have listed for you the ones I think are the most prevalent and the two primary ones most readers will end up using (annual point-to-point and monthly cap).

If you find and review other crediting methods and have questions about them, please feel free to e-mail me at roccy@retiringwithoutrisk.com; and I'd be happy to answer any questions you may have.

PARTICIPATION RATES AND "SPREADS"

The participation rate is the amount of the movement in the index that is credited to the annuity as earnings. The participation rate today in most annual point-to-point crediting FIAs is 100%.

For example: Assume the S&P 500 index increases 12% during the year, but the participation rate in the product is only 80%.

In this case, the annuity would be credited with an earning rate of 9.6% (80% of 12%). If the participation rate was given as 100% but the product had a 9% cap, then the amount credited would be 9% since that is the maximum permitted, or the cap. Sometimes both participation limits and caps are used to determine the earnings credited.

Also, some FIAs employ a fee, generally called the "spread," which is subtracted from the earning rate before it is credited to the annuity. In the foregoing example, if the spread were 2%, the annuity would be credited with 7.6% (9.6% less the 2% spread) and 7% (9% less 2%) respectively.

The participation rates, caps, and spreads may be fixed for a specified time or they may be guaranteed for the term of the annuity. Generally, if they are subject to being reset at the option of the issuer, they will also include minimum and maximum amounts that limit their variability.

The only way for you to determine the variables in a FIA is to carefully analyze it; and if there is still confusion, you should contact an advisor who fully understands the products you are looking at and their variables. I can tell you from experience that many insurance advisors selling FIAs do not fully understand how they work and the various moving parts.

If you cannot find someone in your local area you feel comfortable with who can help you choose the best FIA for your situation, please feel free to contact me (roccy@retiringriskfree.com); and I'll refer you to an advisor who can help you.

SUMMARY ON CREDITING METHODS, CAPS, AND SPREADS

What you need to understand is that there is only so much money to go around when an insurance company constructs a FIA for sale to the general public.

If you ask some of the experts in the field, including me, they will tell you that most of the FIA designs are all supposed to return approximately the same return over time.

While that may be true, one or two of the methods will do better over time; we just don't know which ones at any point in time.

My professional opinion is that an annual point-to-point FIA with a company that is consistent with its caps (meaning the company doesn't lower the caps arbitrarily to increase profits) will be the best crediting method over the long term.

A monthly point-to-point product is really the only one in the market that has significant upside that could possibly not only outperform, but significantly outperform, all of the other crediting methods. Having said that, the monthly point-to-point crediting method could also significantly underperform other crediting methods depending on the volatility of the measuring stock index.

BONUSES

In the last chapter, I touched on premium bonuses. Bonuses can be offered on various types of annuities, but you most often see them on FIAs.

What is a bonus? It's as simple as saying that, when you pay your premium to fund a FIA, the insurance company agrees to credit your cash account value (CAV) with more money than you paid in premium.

If you bought a product that has a 5% premium bonus where your initial premium was $100,000, the cash account value would start out at $105,000.

Therefore, if the S&P 500 index went up 8% in the first year, the 8% would be applied towards the account balance that includes the bonus ($105,000 x 8% = $8,400).

The new CAV for the beginning of year two would be $105,000 + $8,400 = $113,400.

Without the bonus, the beginning year two account balance would be: $100,000 x 8% = $108,000.

Over time, having an annuity with a premium bonus can have a dramatic effect on the cash surrender value (CSV) (which is your walk-away amount when you choose to access cash from the FIA).

Let's look at an example with a 5% premium bonus and a variable return over a 10-year period. The first chart illustrates money growing with **NO** bonus. The second chart illustrates money growing with a **5%** bonus.

Month	Start of Year Balance	Gain or Loss	Year End Index Value	Index Returns
1	**$100,000**	$0	$100,000	-10%
2	$100,000	$5,000	$105,000	5%
3	$105,000	$8,400	$113,400	8%
4	$113,400	$0	$113,400	-4%
5	$113,400	$7,938	$121,338	7%
6	$121,338	$9,707	$131,045	8%
7	$131,045	$7,863	$138,908	6%
8	$138,908	$0	$138,908	-15%
9	$138,908	$6,945	$145,853	5%
10	$145,853	$11,668	$157,521	8%
11	$157,521	$9,451	$166,973	6%
12	$166,973	$0	**$166,973**	-8%

Year	Start of Year Balance	Gain or Loss	Year End Index Value	Index Returns
1	**$105,000**	$0	$105,000	-10%
2	$105,000	$5,250	$110,250	5%
3	$110,250	$8,820	$119,070	8%
4	$119,070	$0	$119,070	-4%
5	$119,070	$8,335	$127,405	7%
6	$127,405	$10,192	$137,597	8%
7	$137,597	$8,256	$145,853	6%
8	$145,853	$0	$145,853	-15%
9	$145,853	$7,293	$153,146	5%
10	$153,146	$12,252	$165,397	8%
11	$165,397	$9,924	$175,321	6%
12	$175,321	$0	**$175,321**	-8%

With this example, the FIA with a 5% bonus had an ending value of **$175,321,** and the FIA with no bonus had a value of **$166,973**.

Based on these numbers, why wouldn't you want an annuity with a bonus?

Good question.

Depending on the company issuing the annuity, the answer may be that there is no reason not to have a bonus.

When a bonus is added to a FIA, one or two things happen.

1) The surrender charge may be increased and lengthened. Basically, the company is willing to give you a bonus because they bank on the fact that most annuity owners will keep their money in the FIA for a longer period of time (at least until the surrender period is over).

If an annuity owner surrenders the FIA early, he/she will typically have a higher than average surrender charge which makes the insurance company whole.

2) The cap on the product may be lower than one without the bonus. This is the one you have to watch out for. I fundamentally don't have a problem with bonus annuities that

increase and lengthen the surrender charge. That is an expense the annuity owner can completely avoid simply by not surrendering the annuity.

However, if the cap is lowered (let's say from 8.5% to 7.5%) because of the bonus, over time that might completely defeat the purpose of the bonus. This is a cost the annuity owner cannot avoid simply by holding the annuity until the end of the surrender period.

Also be aware that some companies have contractual language that forces annuity owners to forfeit some of their bonus if the annuity is surrendered early. Again, I'm not offended by this because it can be avoided by not surrendering the annuity until after the surrender period.

Finally, some companies have contractual language that forces you to take money out of the annuity over a specified period of time in order to benefit by the bonus and the growth on the bonus. If the payment is guaranteed and the annuity owner knows what that payment will be when the time comes to withdraw money from the annuity, I'm okay with that since the annuity purchaser can make an informed decision when purchasing.

If the insurance company dictates that the annuity owner take withdrawals over a certain period of time (let's say 10 years) and does not indicate up front what the income will be, then it becomes much more difficult to know if buying an annuity with a bonus makes sense.

I understand that I'm getting into the real details of the product which some readers will like and some will pass over; but I'll restate that if you have any questions about anything in this book (including whether a bonus annuity makes sense for you), please feel free to e-mail me at roccy@retiringriskfree.com, and I'll do my best to help or to refer you to an advisor in your local area who can help.

WHERE IS THE BEST PLACE TO FIND THE MONEY TO FUND FIAs?

If you'll recall from the last chapter, tax-qualified annuities funded with after-tax dollars allow money to grow tax-deferred.

However, when removing money from an annuity (FIAs included), the money comes out on a first-in, last-out basis. What that means is that your premiums paid (basis) are the last dollars returned to you; and, therefore, the first money returned to you is growth (which is fully income taxable at your income tax bracket when received).

The fact that the gains are taxed is not the end of the world because you did get tax-deferred growth which is good; but if you are going to grow money in an after-tax manner, depending on your age, it may be a better or significantly better idea to grow wealth using cash value life insurance. Remember, with cash inside life insurance, the policy grows tax free and can be removed tax-free in retirement. You can read Chapter 3 to learn the power of growing wealth with cash value life insurance.

Where would I rather see people buy FIAs if they have the option? Inside an IRA or tax-deferred retirement plan.

Why? Because no matter what wealth-building tool you use inside a tax-deferred IRA or qualified retirement plan, all of the money coming out as distributions will be fully taxable at your ordinary income tax bracket at the time of withdrawal.

My opinion on the use of FIAs inside tax deferred IRAs or qualified retirement plans puts me at odds with most CPAs in this country.

Why? Because many CPAs do not understand the reason a client would buy a FIA inside a tax deferred IRA or qualified plan. It's not for the tax deferral (obviously); it's so the money can grow in a protected manner (or as you will read in the next chapter, so the money can grow at a guaranteed rate of return (accumulation value) and provide a guaranteed income for life (something stocks, mutual funds, and bonds cannot provide)).

The next time you talk with a CPA who says it's a bad idea to buy a tax-deferred tool such as a FIA inside a tax deferred IRA or qualified plan, pull out this book and let the CPA read it. After he/she is done, I guarantee you the CPA will come to the conclusion that allocating some amount of money to a FIA will make plenty of sense.

Finally, if you have already or can fund a Roth IRA or 401(k) plan, both are ideal places to buy FIAs. As you know, you fund a Roth IRA or 401(k) plan with after-tax dollars; but once funded, the money can grow tax free and come out tax free. This holds true even if money is funded into FIAs.

DOES BUY AND HOLD WORK IN A VOLATILE STOCK MARKET?

I don't know about you, but most people are a bit freaked out about the stock market. With the stock market crash of 2000-2002 (-46%) and 2007-2009 (-59%), many people are worried about protecting their money and are confused about how to grow their money (which is one of the reasons I decided to write this book).

It is not uncommon today to have days when the stock market is both **up** and **down** nearly **10%**. To say that is volatile is an understatement.

You know what everyone says: "If you are in the market for the "long term," you don't have to worry about the short-term losses."

I suppose that sort of makes sense, doesn't it? Or does it?

This is a new, very volatile world; and the American public needs to find a new way to grow wealth that will help everyone sleep better at night while not missing out on an opportunity to grab investment gains when possible.

This part of the book should really make you rethink how money grows. It should help you determine if buying and holding stocks/mutual funds is always the best thing to do when the stock market is volatile.

Ask yourself this question: "If the stock market goes up and down and up and down over a ten-year period and ends up at the same point ten years from now, will the account balance be the same at the end of the ten-year period"?

If you invested $100,000 in the S&P 500 index which started at, let's say, 1,000 points and if the index went up and down like a yo-yo for ten years and ended with a value of 1,000, would your initial investment still be $100,000?

The answer is <u>NO!</u>

In the chart on the next page, I assumed a very volatile market that goes up and down 10% every six months and after ten years the **<u>average return is ZERO</u>**. What you'll notice is that the account value at the end of the 10-year period is **<u>$95,099</u>** (not $100,000).

<u>Never go backwards</u> and <u>lock in gains</u>

What if you repositioned $100,000 into FIAs instead of mutual funds? If I make a conservative assumption that over time the cap on the FIA returns will be 8% annually, look at the results.

Year S&P500 Index	Initial Investment	Annual	Return	Acct. Value	Initial Investment FIA	Annual	Return	Acct. Balance
End Year 1	$100,000	10%	$10,000	$110,000	$100,000	8.00%	$8,000	$108,000
End Year 2	$110,000	-10%	($11,000)	$99,000	$108,000	0.00%	$0	$108,000
End Year 3	$99,000	10%	$9,900	$108,900	$108,000	8.00%	$8,640	$116,640
End Year 4	$108,900	-10%	($10,890)	$98,010	$116,640	0.00%	$0	$116,640
End Year 5	$98,010	10%	$9,801	$107,811	$116,640	8.00%	$9,331	$125,971
End Year 6	$107,811	-10%	($10,781)	$97,030	$125,971	0.00%	$0	$125,971
End Year 7	$97,030	10%	$9,703	$106,733	$125,971	8.00%	$10,078	$136,049
End Year 8	$106,733	-10%	($10,673)	$96,060	$136,049	0.00%	$0	$136,049
End Year 9	$96,060	10%	$9,606	$105,666	$136,049	8.00%	$10,884	$146,933
End Year 10	$105,666	-10%	($10,567)	$95,099	$146,933	0.00%	$0	$146,933
Ave.Return		0.00%				4.00%		

Why did the FIA end up with an account balance of **$146,933** instead of **$95,099**? Simple—in down years the FIA returned ZERO instead of **-10%**, and in up years it returned **8%**.

By the way, I assumed no mutual fund expenses in the above example. If I added a **1.2% mutual fund expense**, the $95,099 ending account balance would have been **$84,180**.

Are these examples real world? Prior to 1999, you would have said no way? Are these examples real world? Who knows, they could be. The question of the day is: "Are you doing everything you can to help protect your money in this uncertain world?"

It's one thing to be upset when you only earned **8%** when the market is up **10%+**; it's another and much more positive feeling when your money earns ZERO when the market is down **10%+**.

The first feeling makes you a little grumpy; but the second, even though it sounds odd to be happy with a ZERO rate of return, brings a nice smile to your face (especially if you are over the age of 60-65 and close to or in retirement).

Just in case you are curious, if the market has wild swings of **20%** every other year (up and down), the account balance at the end of 10 years would be **$81,537*** and the FIA account balance would remain at **$146,933**. *This number does not include a 1.2% mutual fund expense.

SUMMARY ON BUYING AND HOLDING IN THE STOCK MARKET

I'm not sure if the days of "buy and hold" have come and gone as a tried and true way of growing your wealth. That may or may not be the case. What I know is that it's time for you to understand ALL the various options to grow and protect your wealth, and I hope this information has been helpful.

WHO ARE THE MOST LIKELY CANDIDATES TO USE FIAs TO GROW WEALTH?

A better question is who is NOT a candidate to use FIAs to grow their wealth. Let me list who I believe are **not** the ideal candidates to use FIAs to grow their wealth.

1) People who need a lot of liquidity with the money that could be allocated to the FIA.

While surrender charges typically range from 5%-15% depending on the FIA purchased and last typically less than 12 years, if you know you may need the money, a FIA may not be suitable for you. However, there is also the ability to take a 10% annual free withdrawal (and 20% as a one-time amount with some companies); but again, if much or most of the money may be needed in liquid form, then using a FIA to grow wealth will not be a good fit.

2) Anyone looking to access the funds prior to age 59½ years old.

Remember, tax-deferred annuities are similar to qualified-retirement plans and IRAs in that there is a 10% penalty from the IRA if you take money out prior to age 59½.

This can be avoided by taking a systematic income stream vs. the ability to take a lump-sum withdrawal; but as a general rule, again, if you need access to the funds prior to age 59½ years old, building wealth in a FIA may not be an appropriate place.

3) If you like action in the stock market and the potential to average 10-12-14%+ a year in a brokerage account, you are not a candidate for growing wealth with a FIA.

I almost laugh at the above numbers due to the fact that from 1998-2008 the S&P 500 index averaged 8.35% and the average investor earned only 1.87%. My point being that there are few investors who have actually been able to earn 10-12-14%+. However, if you are one who would like to try to beat the market, you are not a candidate for FIAs.

4) If you are under the age of 60 and can systematically fund X amount of dollars into a cash value life insurance policy, you may not be a candidate to grow wealth in a FIA.

Cash value life insurance can be a much better wealth-accumulation tool, and it is a more tax-favorable wealth-building tool due to the fact that money can be removed from a policy income tax free.

Additionally, when you die using cash value life insurance to grow wealth, a nice death benefit will pass to the heirs in an income and possibly estate tax free manner.

-If you do not fall into one of the above categories, then you are probably a good candidate to grow wealth using a FIA.

-If you like the idea of receiving a guaranteed rate of return (accumulation value) of 4-7%+ coupled with a guaranteed income for life, then you are a candidate for a FIA (see the next chapter).

-If you like to sleep at night and not worry about the stock market crashing, you are a candidate for FIAs.

-If you like the idea of receiving a free long-term care benefit, you are a candidate for FIAs.

The bottom line is that FIAs are a tremendously powerful and protective wealth-building tool that most readers of this book once they learn the power wish they'd used over the last 10-20 years.

FIAs will not bring us world peace or solve all of our problems. However, when it comes to growing wealth with no downside risk where the gains are locked in every year and can never be lost due to a downturn in the stock market, FIAs can play an integral role in wealth-building/retirement plans of millions of Americans.

GUARANTEED RETURNS COUPLED WITH A GUARANTEED INCOME FOR LIFE

Some people who read this chapter will find it interesting and motivating to the point of seeking out more information and an advisor who can help them with FIAs.

Some people who read this chapter will find it interesting and not quite motivating enough to seek out more information with the thought of a possible purchase (mainly because of the caps on earnings).

For those who this chapter didn't motivate, I hope to cure that with the next chapter where I will show you how with the "right" FIA you can earn a **guaranteed rate of return** (accumulation value) of 4-7+% depending on the FIA purchased coupled with a **guaranteed income for life**.

If that doesn't motivate you to learn more about FIA annuities, nothing will.

So, let's move on to the next exciting chapter where you can learn how these guarantees work.

Chapter 7
Earn a Guaranteed Return with a Guaranteed Income for Life

For many readers, this chapter may be the most important chapter of any book you've ever read.

What you will learn in this chapter will truly amaze you. The possibilities that await you when it comes to growing your wealth in a guaranteed (accumulation value) wealth-building tool that will also provide for you a guaranteed income for life you can NEVER outlive will truly blow your mind.

Let me ask you a few simple questions that will set up this chapter:

1) What's more important to you today when deciding how to grow your wealth?

-Reaching for 8-10-12%+ growth where your money is **100% at risk** to stock market downturns and crashes?

OR

-Earning a **7% guaranteed** return (on accumulating assets)?

2) In retirement, would you be happy if your accumulated assets could **guarantee** an income stream you could never outlive with the following schedule:

5% if activated at age 60

6% if activated at age 70

7% if activated at age 80

If you would be happy with a guaranteed return on your wealth coupled with a guaranteed income stream that you could never outlive, then you should proceed to read the rest of this chapter.

If you like the concept of placing 100% of your liquid wealth **at risk** in the stock market in an effort to generate returns that could be 8-10-12%+ or produce returns of -59% (like what happened in 2007-2009), then you do not need to read this chapter.

HOW DO YOU RECEIVE A GUARANTEED RETURN COUPLED WITH A GUARANTEED INCOME FOR LIFE?

The first question that needs to be answered is "what investment firm, bank, or other entity is going to give someone a guaranteed rate of return and a guaranteed income for life?"

The answer is that **life insurance companies** offer products with such guarantees when a consumer purchases a particular type of annuity coupled with a Guaranteed Income for Life Benefit (GIB) "**rider**."

A rider is a contractual option that is added onto an insurance product to add one or more features/benefits to the base product.

Therefore, in answer to the question used for the heading of this section of the book, the answer is that, in order to receive a guaranteed rate of return coupled with a guaranteed income for life, you need to **buy an annuity** from a life insurance company and then add to that product a **GIB rider**.

HOW LONG HAVE GIB RIDERS BEEN AROUND?

Surprisingly, GIBs (also known as GMIB in the securities industry) have been around for years. Until recently, this rider was only available on a variable annuity (vs. a fixed indexed annuity).

The reason you might not have heard of a GIB rider on an annuity is because few advisors sell them.

Let me rephrase that; prior to the 2000-2002 stock market crash, few advisors sold GIB riders with annuity sales. After the stock market's most recent crash in 2007-2009, many more advisors are selling annuities with GIB riders.

VARIABLE ANNUITIES VS. FIXED INDEXED ANNUITIES

As I just indicated, until recently, you could only purchase a GIB rider on a variable annuity (VA). However, in the last few years, fixed indexed annuities (FIAs) have started to offer a GIB rider; and that's good for the American consumer. Why? Because the American consumer is clamoring for guaranteed income products, and they want to buy such products in a non-variable environment.

This book is not a dissertation on the differences between VAs and FIAs and which GIB rider is better.

I have already written a **33-page white paper** on this subject for use in the financial services industry, and I can state with confidence that the GIB riders offered on most FIAs are far superior to those offered on VAs.

If you already have been or in the future are approached by an advisor touting the virtues of VAs and GIB riders, you will need to be armed with the knowledge imparted to those who read my 33-page white paper. If you would like a copy of the white paper, you can download it by going to www.retiringwithoutrisk.com.

For the remainder of this chapter, I will be using the assumption (based on mathematical facts) that GIB riders on FIAs are better than those offered on VAs; and, therefore, I will only be addressing GIB riders in the context of a FIA.

GIB RIDERS—GETTING STARTED

Let me start with the basics for how you would go about obtaining a guaranteed income for life you can never outlive.

You first have to choose to buy a FIA with an insurance company that offers a GIB rider on its products.

When purchasing the annuity, you will decide if you would like to add to the annuity a GIB rider (I will discuss and illustrate the expenses of the rider in an upcoming section). You must add the rider at the time you purchase the FIA.

The FIA may be one with a bonus, a monthly cap, annual point-to-point cap, or other varying design features. The GIB rider is an add on to a FIA so your variety of annuities that can be purchased with the rider is quite diverse.

You pay your premiums to the insurance company which, in turn, funds the FIA just as it would any FIA.

However, if you choose to add on a GIB rider, the accounting in a FIA is dramatically different than a FIA without the rider.

ACCUMULATION ACCOUNT VALUE VS. ACTUAL ACCOUNT VALUE

With any FIA, the annuity owner will have a **cash account value** (CAV) (the amount of money actually growing at market rates in the annuity every year) and a **cash surrender value** (CSV) (the amount of money an owner would walk away with if he/she surrendered the annuity and asked for all the available cash). I discussed the CAV and CSV in Chapter 5 on Annuities.

When a GIB rider is added to a FIA, there is an additional accounting measure that must take place. The insurance company must start an accounting for what I like to call the "**accumulation account value**" (AAV).

The AAV is the amount that will increase at whatever the guarantee being offered by the insurance company happens to be at the time you buy the annuity with a GIB rider. If you bought a FIA with a 7% "guaranteed" return, the guarantee is applied only towards the AAV NOT the CAV or CSV (see the following example for a better understanding of the distinction).

The AAV is **NOT a walk-away account value**. It is **ONLY used for calculation purposes** when determining the guaranteed income for life payment.

Let me use an example, and I think you'll understand how the two different account values grow. In the following chart, you will see an AAV in the center column and the actual account value in the right-hand column (for this example, assume the actual account value is the CAV).

This example product has a **7% guaranteed rate of return** every year on the AAV. For the CAV, I assumed a random rate of return (which is what will happen in the real world).

	Accumulation Account Value	Cash Account Value
Issue Age 55	$100,000	$100,000
Year 1 Age 56	$107,000	$103,600
Year 2 Age 57	$114,490	$107,329
Year 3 Age 58	$122,504	$111,193
Year 4 Age 59	$131,080	$115,196
Year 5 Age 60	$140,255	$119,343
Year 6 Age 61	$150,073	$123,639
Year 7 Age 62	$160,578	$128,090
Year 8 Age 63	$171,819	$132,702
Year 9 Age 64	$183,846	$137,479
Year 10 Age 65	**$196,715**	**$142,428**

As you can see, the center column grows at 7% and is much higher than the actual account value in the right-hand column. While one of my favorite FIAs did grow on average more than 6% over the last ten years (1998-2008), I wanted to assume something less for this example.

The previous example assumes **NO surrender charge**. I created this no surrender charge example so you could simply see the difference between the actual account value and the accumulation account value

Now let me show you what it would look with the surrender charges.

	Accumulation Account Value	Cash Account Value	Cash Surrender Value
Issue Age 55	$100,000	$100,000	$90,000
Year 1 Age 56	$107,000	$103,600	$94,276
Year 2 Age 57	$114,490	$107,329	$98,743
Year 3 Age 58	$122,504	$111,193	$103,409
Year 4 Age 59	$131,080	$115,196	$108,284
Year 5 Age 60	$140,255	$119,343	$113,376
Year 6 Age 61	$150,073	$123,639	$118,693
Year 7 Age 62	$160,578	$128,090	$124,247
Year 8 Age 63	$171,819	$132,702	$130,048
Year 9 Age 64	$183,846	$137,479	$136,104
Year 10 Age 65	**$196,715**	**$142,428**	**$142,428**

Remember that virtually all annuities have surrender charges. In this example, if you wanted to surrender (get rid of) this annuity, you would receive what's in the right-hand column.

You'll notice that in year ten the CAV and the CSV are exactly the same. That means that the surrender charge period is over after ten years.

What you should also know is that, when you buy a FIA with a GIB rider, you can typically activate it 12 months after purchase and NOT have the surrender charge affect the guaranteed income benefit.

MINI-SUMMARY

When you buy a FIA with a GIB rider, your FIA will start with three account values.

The accumulation account value is ONLY used to calculate the guaranteed income benefit (discussed in an upcoming section).

If you want access to all of your cash, you will be given the cash surrender value which in my example is the same as the cash account value starting in year ten.

The <u>cash account value</u> is the actual account value as the money grows every year in the FIA and is the amount that would pass to your heirs at death.

You can start your guaranteed income benefit while the FIA is still in the surrender charge period; doing so has NO effect on your GIB for life.

ACCUMULATION PERIOD

FIA products vary on the period of time each will allow money to grow at the guaranteed rate. Most companies allow the money to grow in the accumulation account for no longer than 10 years.

Some companies allow 12-15 years and some 20.

One company allows for accumulation up to age 90, but it is a bit of a hybrid product that I don't care for; and so I will not discuss it in this book.

Why is there a limit on the number of years most insurance companies will allow the guaranteed account to accumulate?

Without getting too technical, it has to do with the cash reserves that the companies must set aside in order to guarantee the return. The longer the guaranteed accumulation period the more cash the insurance company has to set aside in a reserve account.

When an insurance company does not plan properly and has to allocate too much money to its reserves to cover the guarantees of these products, it hurts the company's ability to grow and its flexibility. Recently, a few companies sold so many FIAs with the GIB rider that one day the companies literally stopped taking in new clients and new money (almost unheard of in the insurance business).

Therefore, while a FIA with a GIB rider is an absolutely unique and wonderfully protective wealth-building tool, if you are too young, you are not going to add the rider on to a FIA until you know with some certainty that you will activate the rider by the end of the accumulation period (which again, with most products is 10 years).

As far as activation is concerned, as I stated, with most products you can activate the GIB rider 12 months after purchasing the annuity. When you reach the point where the GIB will no longer accumulate because you are over the number of years for the guarantee, you are not required to activate the rider. You'd be crazy if you didn't activate it because you will no longer be receiving a guaranteed roll up, but you do not have to activate the rider.

WITHDRAWAL VS. ANNUITIZATION

One of the unique features of a GIB for life rider with a FIA is that it does NOT require annuitization. An annuitant can activate an income stream for life; but if he/she needs a lump sum of money, the money in the actual account value will be available. Withdrawals will decrease future payment streams or will cause them to cease if all of the remaining actual account value is withdrawn.

When you take a withdrawal from a FIA with a GIB rider, you are taking the withdrawal from the <u>actual account value</u> not the <u>guaranteed accumulation account value</u>.

Let me give you an example of how taking a withdrawal can affect your income benefit. Assume you had $100,000 in your actual account value. If you had a need for $50,000 and removed that from your FIA, if you were to start your GIB for life benefit, your income stream would be reduced by 50% (which almost seems too logical).

The ability to withdraw money from a FIA after the GIB rider has been activated is very important because "in the old days" the only way to receive a guaranteed income for life was through the use of a Single Premium Immediate Annuity (SPIA). SPIAs have no cash value and, therefore, you're stuck and have no access to the cash in the annuity. Also, most of the time with a FIA that has a GIB rider, the annuity owner's heirs will receive more or even much more as a death benefit than with a SPIA.

CALCULATING THE GUARANTEED LIFETIME INCOME STREAM

What a comforting and terrific concept to discuss. A guaranteed lifetime income you can never outlive. How many Americans wished they had their money in a product like this prior to the recent -59% downturn in the stock market?

The first thing you need to know is that different insurance companies have different ways they calculate the GIB. The basics of how the income is calculated are the same, but the amount of payments per company can vary.

The second thing you need to know/remember is that the GIB is based off the **guaranteed accumulation account value**.

How does the GIB for life payment work?

Before I explain the math behind how a GIB rider works, let me state that it's not the easiest thing in the world to calculate these numbers. In fact, when you are trying to compare the different riders at multiple companies, it's very difficult.

Because of the difficulty of calculating the numbers, I paid programmers to create my own proprietary software application that allows me to calculate the GIB with virtually any GIB rider.

It is my guess that many readers of this book will be curious as to how much income for life can be generated using a GIB rider. As such and because my proprietary calculator itself is not too difficult to use, I have made the calculator available online for readers of my book to use on a trial basis. To sign up to use my GIB calculator, simply go to www.retiringwithoutrisk.com and click on the appropriate link to sign up.

How does the GIB for life payment work? It's really quite simple. When you decide to activate the GIB for life, the insurance company takes the guaranteed accumulation account value (AAV) at that time and then pays you a percentage of income based on that account value for life.

An example will crystallize how it works.

Assume you are 70 years old when you activate the GIB for life rider. Also assume that the guaranteed AAV is $500,000 at that time. Finally, assume that your FIA contract with the insurance carrier states that at age 70 you will be paid a guaranteed income benefit for life based on a rate of 6%.

The math would look as follows:

$500,000 x .6% = **$30,000**.

Therefore, you would be paid an income benefit of $30,000 every year until you died. If you died early, there will be an account balance that passes to your heirs (discussed in an upcoming section). If you live until the ripe old age of 100+, the insurance company will keep on paying you.

VARIOUS GIB PAYMENT SCHEUDLES

As I indicated, GIB rider terms offered by different companies in the marketplace may vary.

Most companies use the following payment schedule:

5% if the rider is activated before age 70

6% before age 80

7% before age 90

8% at age 90 and over

Some companies use the following schedule:

5% if the rider is activated before age 65

5.5% if activated at ages 65-69

6% if activated at ages 70-74

6.5% if activated at ages 75-79

7% if activated at ages 80-84

7.5% if activated at ages 85-89

8% at age 90 and over

The "fairest" payment schedule

At least one company in the marketplace has a payment schedule that is calculated by taking the annuitant's age at the time of activation and subtracting 10. It sounds simple enough.

5% if the rider is activated at age 60

5.3% if activate at age 63

6.7% if activated at age 77

7.4% if activated at age 84

8% if activated at age 90

The maximum income varies per company but ranges from 7-8% typically.

As you will see, there is a significant difference between the typical payment schedule and the fairest payment schedule.

Example 1

Let's look at an example for a 79 year old with $500,000 in his FIA accumulation account with a GIB for life rider. With some products in the marketplace, the client is going to receive a GIB of **6%** a year for life.

The income for this annuitant using a normal FIA with a GIB rider would be $30,000 a year ($500,000 x 6%).

What about with the fairer GIB payout? The example client would receive a GIB of **6.9%** (79 (age) – 10 = 69 x .001 = 6.9%).

The income for this annuitant using what I consider the FIA with the fairest GIB for life rider (6.9%) payment schedule would be $34,500 a year. With the better payment percentage, the annuitant receives **$4,500 more** income every year for life. If the annuitant lived another 10 years, that's an additional $45,000 of income.

DIFFERENT GUARANTEED RETURN PERCENTAGES

Example 2

This example will use the information from a previous example and will illustrate how important both the guaranteed rate of return on the accumulation account is and the guaranteed rate of return on the income benefit.

There is a significant difference between a guaranteed accumulation value of **5%** and **7%**. For example, if a client, age 50, positioned $500,000 into the new FIA with a 7% guaranteed accumulation value, that value at age 70 would be **$1,934,842**.

If the client used a FIA with a guaranteed accumulation value of 5%, that value would be **1,326,649**.

There is also a significant difference when an annuitant can receive an income benefit of **5.9%** vs. **5%**.

If an example client is 69 when starting the GIB, using the more client friendly FIA, the GIB for life would be 5.9% x $1,934,842 (the accumulation value) = **$114,155** every year until death.

Using the typical or more standard income payment schedule which is a 5% income benefit ($1,943,842 x 5%), the annual payment for life would be **$96,742**.

When I compare that to the typical payment schedule using a 5% guarantee on the accumulation account and a 5.9% GIB, look at the difference:

5.9% x $1,326,649 = **$78,272** every year until death. Using a 5% income benefit on the 5% guaranteed roll-up accumulation account, the payment each year would be **$66,332**.

The difference is staggering. The following chart brings all the previous numbers together. You'll notice the biggest difference in annual payments is between a 7% guaranteed return with 5.9% payout and the 5% guaranteed return with 5% payout.

	5.9% Income	5% income
7% Guaranteed Return (accumulation account)	$114,155	$96,742
5% Guaranteed Return (accumulation account)	$78,272	$66,332
Difference in income for a 15 year payout for a 70 year old	**$538,245**	**$456,150**

The point with these example is not to confuse you (which some of you may be). The point is how vitally important it is to find the product with the **highest guaranteed rate of return** on the accumulation value as well as the **highest guaranteed income rate of return**.

Finally, most FIAs also have a reset feature in them. If over a time frame (typically five years) the actual account value returns in a FIA are greater than the guaranteed rate of return on the accumulation account value, the accumulation account value will be reset to the higher value.

WHEN IS A 7% GUARANTEED RATE OF RETURN BETTER THAN AN 8%?

To further illustrate the problems consumers may have when picking a product, I want to explain a classic marketing technique that some companies employ in the sales process.

If I asked you if you would rather have an 8% or 7% guaranteed rate of return on an accumulation value for a FIA, what would you say? Of course, you'd say 8%.

When is a 7% guaranteed return better than an 8% guarantee?

The simple answer is when the GIB from the 7% guaranteed return product is better than the 8% guaranteed return product. How can that be? You may have guessed the two ways by what you've already read.

1) The GIB rate of return for the 7% guaranteed return product (accumulation value) may be higher. For example, the income benefit may be 1% higher with the 7% product which, in turn, over a lifetime of the payments could overcome the fact that

the accumulation account upon which the GIB is based is lower than the 8% product.

2) The accumulation period for the 7% guaranteed return product may be 5-10 years longer than that of the 8% guaranteed return product.

Let's look at an example where the roll-up period for one annuity is 10 years and one is 20 years. I'm also going to throw into the mix that the 7% product uses the fairer guaranteed income payment schedule. Assume the annuitant was 50 years old when he/she funding both annuities.

Income at Age	Fairer Payment Schedule	GIB w/ 7% Roll-up up to 20-years	Typical Payment Schedule	Income w/ 8% Roll-up up to 10-years
60	5%	$9,835	5%	$10,794
64	5.40%	$13,924	5%	$10,794
65	5.50%	$15,174	5.50%	$11,874
69	5.90%	$21,337	5.50%	$11,874

What do you notice about the previous chart?

Look at the percentage used to generate the guaranteed income at the various ages. At age 60, both companies have a 5% income benefit.

At age **64**, the fairer FIA has a **5.4%** income benefit and the other product still has a **5%** income benefit.

Therefore, unless the annuity owner activates his/her income stream right at age 60, the income from the FIA with the fairer payment schedule will be higher.

Now let's look at age **65** and **69**. There is a huge income difference in the two products. Why?

Because the 7% FIA in this example has a **guaranteed 20-year accumulation roll up**. The 8% FIA has a **10-year accumulation roll up**. In year 11, there is no guarantee of 8% (I've assumed the worst case scenario that could happen which is no growth due to a low account value over the first 10 years).

Is the previous example a manipulated one? Absolutely. I intentionally manipulated it to drive home the point that is vitally important that annuity owners understand how these products work so they are not taken in by flashy sales techniques. With a good understanding of how these products work, potential annuity buyers can pick the one that best fits their situation.

SUMMARY ON ROLL UP GUARANTEES AND VARIOUS INCOME-FOR-LIFE PERCENTAGES

If I thoroughly confused you with all the numbers from the previous pages, let me explain in a simple summary what I'm trying to get across.

Many companies that sell guaranteed income for life benefit riders have different terms.

-Some companies have their products priced to be very aggressive with a high guaranteed rate of return on the accumulation account.

-Some companies have their products priced so that, when you are in the payment phase of the product, the payment schedule is the "fairest."

-Some companies try to not have the best guaranteed income rate of return or the best income for life terms but have average terms for both aspects of the guarantee.

Remember, there is only so much money to go around in these products.

If one company has an 8% guaranteed rate of return, the chances are that the payment percentage may be lower than other products with a more spread out age bracket for when the income percentage increases.

The opposite may be true if the guaranteed income terms are much more favorable than other products in the marketplace.

What it really comes down to is "suitability." You need to find the best product that fits your needs.

-Do you want to turn the income on after 12 months?

-Do you want to let the money grow at the guaranteed rate for as long as possible?

-Or maybe you don't know at the time you are funding the FIA and, therefore, you may choose to pick a product that has middle-of-the-road numbers for both the guaranteed income and the payout percentage.

Do I realistically believe the average consumer can make this decision on his/her own?

Actually, the answer is yes IF you were able to find all the quality products in the marketplace (which would be very difficult).

Therefore, you'll most likely be relying on an advisor for help. As you read in the Foreword, picking an advisor who knows what he/she is doing with this subject matter can be difficult.

If you are having problems finding someone you feel comfortable with or don't want to go through the interview process with several advisors you don't know, feel free to e-mail me at roccy@retiringwithoutrisk.com; and I'd be happy to refer you to someone in your local area who can help you (or you can go to www.retiringwithoutrisk.com and fill out a form to ask for help or a referral).

COST OF THE GIB RIDER

It would be nice if the insurance companies added guaranteed benefit income riders (GIBs) for free with their annuities. Unfortunately, that is not the case.

Having said that, it is my understanding that some of the insurance companies that offer GIB riders price them at their "cost." By cost, I mean that the insurance company is not trying to make any money on the rider. Instead, the company is offering the rider simply as an enticement for consumers to buy it.

The GIB for life rider for FIAs varies per company. Some are as low as .40% a year and some go as high as .85% a year.

As you know, the account balance in a FIA cannot go backwards due to market declines. However, it **can go backwards** if this rider is added and the FIA has a return of zero in any particular year (a return of zero happens when the S&P 500 has a negative return or if, by chance, the index actually returns zero).

The fee for the GIB for life rider is taken out of the account value **every year** regardless of the returns.

HOW CAN INSURANCE COMPANIES AFFORD TO GIVE YOU A GUARANTEED RETURN AND A GUARANTEED PAYMENT FOR LIFE?

This question has probably been in the back of your mind as you've been reading this chapter. It had me scratching my head for a few minutes until I fully researched how these products are priced.

Remember that with a FIA the product is already designed to never have its account value go backwards due to negative market rates of return. Additionally, the gains are locked in annually.

Therefore, unlike variable products that can literally lose 59%+ of their value within a short time frame, an insurance company issuing a FIA does not.

THE GIB PAYMENTS ARE COMING FROM YOUR OWN FIA ACCOUNT

When the insurance company starts paying you a lifetime income stream, it is taking the money from your own FIA's actual account value. In essence, the insurance company is **giving you back your own money**.

You may think that removing money from your actual account value will quickly reduce the account value; but remember, the actual account value will still grow in years when the measuring stock index is positive with those gains locking in (which reduces the speed at which the account value is diminished).

Additionally, the insurance company has priced the product with the additional rider fee (.40%-.85%) annually to help make sure the product is profitable.

Let's look at the actual numbers from an example so you don't have to take my word for it. I'm going to use an example where the assumed rate of return is 5% annually on the actual account value and where a 60-yearold client waits until age 70 to start his/her income stream.

The upcoming chart is the largest chart in the book. I've left it long (vs. only showing every five years) because I think it is very helpful when understanding how a GIB rider works. You'll notice that the right hand column title is: 'To heirs at death." I've discussed what will pass to the heirs upon death but not given you a visual.

As I briefly alluded to before, in the "old days" one of the only ways to receive a guaranteed income benefit for life was to buy a Single Premium Immediate Annuity (SPIA). A SPIA is typically designed to pay for a set period (such as 10 years) or for someone's lifetime. The kicker is that, if you live past ten years and die, your heirs usually get nothing. As you will see in the following chart, there is an account balance that will pass to the heirs into the 19th year of payment.

If the example client bought a SPIA for comparison sakes, it would have been purchased at age 70 due to the fact that that is when he would start an income-for-life payment.

What you'll also notice in the following chart is the fee for the GIB rider. It will be painful to look at; but if you want to put it into perspective, if Mr. Smith had his money in a typical mutual fund that would give him NO downside protection in the market (let alone a 7% guaranteed return on an accumulation account), the average mutual fund expense would be 2-3 times that of the fee for the GIB rider.

Also, with this example, I assumed the product purchased had a 5% bonus (which is why the beginning account balance is $525,000 when the initial premium is $500,000).

And, finally, you'll notice with a big smile on your face how, if you happen to live a long and happy life like this example client, the income-for-life payment continues for years after the actual account balance goes to zero.

Age	Start of Year Balance	Income for Life	Growth	Fee	To heirs at Death
60	$525,000	$0	$26,250	$2,756	**$548,494**
61	$548,494	$0	$27,425	$2,880	**$573,039**
62	$573,039	$0	$28,652	$3,008	**$598,682**
63	$598,682	$0	$29,934	$3,143	**$625,473**
64	$625,473	$0	$31,274	$3,284	**$653,463**
65	$653,463	$0	$32,673	$3,431	**$682,706**
66	$682,706	$0	$34,135	$3,584	**$713,257**
67	$713,257	$0	$35,663	$3,745	**$745,175**
68	$745,175	$0	$37,259	$3,912	**$778,522**
69	$778,522	$0	$38,926	$4,087	**$813,361**
70	$813,361	$61,965	$37,570	$3,945	**$785,020**
71	$785,020	$61,965	$36,153	$3,796	**$755,412**
72	$755,412	$61,965	$34,672	$3,641	**$724,478**
73	$724,478	$61,965	$33,126	$3,478	**$692,160**
74	$692,160	$61,965	$31,510	$3,309	**$658,396**
75	$658,396	$61,965	$29,822	$3,131	**$623,121**
76	$623,121	$61,965	$28,058	$2,946	**$586,268**
77	$586,268	$61,965	$26,215	$2,753	**$547,765**
78	$547,765	$61,965	$24,290	$2,550	**$507,539**
79	$507,539	$61,965	$22,279	$2,339	**$465,513**
80	$465,513	$61,965	$20,177	$2,119	**$421,607**
81	$421,607	$61,965	$17,982	$1,888	**$375,736**
82	$375,736	$61,965	$15,689	$1,647	**$327,812**
83	$327,812	$61,965	$13,292	$1,396	**$277,743**
84	$277,743	$61,965	$10,789	$1,133	**$225,434**
85	$225,434	$61,965	$8,173	$858	**$170,784**
86	$170,784	$61,965	$5,441	$571	**$113,688**
87	$113,688	$61,965	$2,586	$272	**$54,037**
88	$54,037	$61,965	$0	$0	**$0**
89	$0	$61,965	$0	$0	**$0**
90	$0	$61,965	$0	$0	**$0**
95	$0	$61,965	$0	$0	**$0**
100	$0	$61,965	$0	$0	**$0**

I personally do not think the fees outlined in the previous chart are outrageous at all. As I indicated, if you had your money in a typical mutual fund with an annual expense of 1.5% every year, the fee would be nearly three times what the GIB rider fee is for a FIA.

In case you wondered, the total fees in the previous 39-year example to guarantee a rate of return (accumulation value) of 7% with a guaranteed income of $61,965 for the rest of your life you can never outlive are $75,000.

If you had your money in an average mutual fund that offers you NO guaranteed return and NO guaranteed income for life (but does put 100% of your money at risk in the stock market every day), the fees over the life of the plan would be **$226,804**.

For my money, I'd rather pay $75,000 in fees to have a guaranteed rate of return that is used to pay me a guaranteed income for life vs. a $226,804 fee to keep my money in mutual funds that places my money at risk to <u>59%</u> market downturns like we saw at a period of time from 2007-2009.

While you may not want to pay the fee, as I explain in the following section, I believe the decision to add a GIB rider to a FIA is not a very difficult decision to make if you are in the right age bracket to activate it by the end of the guaranteed accumulation period.

DOES IT MAKE FINANCIAL SENSE TO ADD A GIB RIDER TO A FIA?

This is a question not asked much in the insurance and financial services fields. The insurance companies definitely do not talk about it; and most agents do not have the ability to run the numbers to determine, given certain fact patterns, if adding a GIB rider makes sense.

To determine if adding the rider makes sense, I need to walk through an example and illustrate when it will and when it won't make sense.

The main **variable** when determining if the GIB will make financial sense to add to a FIA is what rate the actual account value will grow at while the owner is still living. If the actual rate of return in the FIA is high enough, then it will not make sense for someone to purchase the rider (from a pure financial point of view).

Of course, we have no idea when we are going to die which is why people buy GIB riders (so they will NEVER run out of money no matter when they die).

Having said that, I know that anytime a consumer thinks about an annual fee (mutual fund expense, money management fee, or GIB rider fee) that is charged every year, usually the consumer wants to know if it makes financial sense to pay the fee if "real-world" assumptions are used.

Example 1: Assume the example client, Mr. Smith, is 60 years old and has $500,000 in an IRA as his main asset that he needs to use to pay his expenses until death.

He is considering a FIA because of the protective features of the product, but he wonders if the expense of the rider makes sense. Mr. Smith does not intend to start his GIB for 10 years; and the product he is looking at has a 5% bonus, a 7% guaranteed rate of return, and would pay him a 6% income benefit at age 70.

Further assume the GIB rider fee is .5% a year.

If the **actual** (not guaranteed) average rate of return in the FIA is **5% a year**, when would the actual account value go to zero?

FYI, the guaranteed income stream every year for life for Mr. Smith at age 70 would be **$61,965**.

With the .5% GIB rider expense, the actual account value in the FIA would go to zero at age **88**.

Without the .5% GIB rider expense, the actual account value would go to zero at age **91**.

What if the returns in the actual account value only averaged a return of **4% a year**?

With the .5% GIB rider expense, the actual account value in the FIA would go to zero at age **84**.

Without the .5% GIB rider expense, the actual account value would go to zero at age **86**.

Conclusion for Example 1: If Mr. Smith has "reasonable" returns in his FIA and dies when he's supposed to from an actuarial point of view (age 85), he doesn't need the GIB rider.

However, if I were giving advice to Mr. Smith, would I recommend as his advisor that he buy the GIB rider? Absolutely.

We are living longer than ever these days; and for the minor cost of the rider, he can guarantee that he will NEVER run out of money no matter how long he lives. I would feel terrible if I gave him any other kind of advice if he actually lived until age 88+ and ran out of money (at a time when his expenses could be very high due to medical costs).

Example 2: Assume the same as Example 1, except Mr. Smith is now 69 years old and he is planning on starting his income payments when he turns 70.

Assume the returns in the actual account value averaged a return of **5% a year**?

With the .5% GIB rider expense, the actual account value in the FIA would go to zero at age **97**.

Without the .5% GIB rider expense, the actual account value would go to zero at age **100**.

From this example, you might think that I would not recommend the GIB rider because without the fee the FIA would not run out of money until age 100. Right? The answer is maybe. I would still be inclined to recommend the rider. Why?

Let's look at what would happen if Mr. Smith did not earn "average" returns in the FIA.

Let me first assume that the FIA only generates a return of **3% a year** in the actual account value. The actual account value would run out of money at age 90.

The bottom line is we have no idea what the stock market will return over the next 10-20-30+ year, and we have no idea how long we will live.

I fundamentally don't have a problem with someone rolling the dice on when they will run out of money; I just don't want to be the advisor giving the advice.

TIME FRAME TO ACTIVATE THE GIB RIDER

As briefly stated earlier, a GIB rider on most FIAs can usually be activated anytime after owning the annuity for 12 months. However, the annuitant for most FIAs must be age 60 or older to activate it.

ENHANCED INCOME BENEFIT

Some FIAs will provide an increased income benefit that acts like a **long-term care benefit** (LTC).

LTC insurance policies typically activate and pay benefits when you can't perform two of your six ADLs (Activities of Daily Living: eating, bathing, dressing, toileting, transferring (walking), and continence).

The best enhanced benefit I know of in the marketplace adds 3% to the guaranteed income stream. Therefore, if an annuitant is 70 years old, the normal income stream would typically be 6%. If the annuitant can't perform two of six ADLs, that income stream would be **increased to 9%**. The maximum I've seen in the marketplace is an enhanced income payment with an **11% annual payout**.

This enhanced benefit on some FIAs is FREE.

SIMPLE INTEREST VS. COMPOUNDING INTEREST

There are some products on the market that guarantee you a rate of return on the accumulation account but instead pay the guarantee using a simple interest rate, not one that compounds.

Some see this tactic as a bit of a marketing ploy (which I suppose it can be). Obviously, if a company is paying based on a simple rate of return, the return can be higher. Therefore, you'll see simple-interest products advertised at higher or even much higher guaranteed rates of return. You might even respond to one of these ads only to find out that the rate is, in fact, a simple one and not compound.

Does that mean there is no place for a simple interest rate-of-return product? Not necessarily. Look at the following numbers. The numbers in the right column are growing at an 8% simple rate of return, and the center column is growing at a 7% compounding rate.

For someone who is going to start the income stream in the first few years, a simple rate-of-return product might make sense.

Year	Age	Year End Balance 7% compound	Year End Balance 8% Simple
1	60	$115,560	$116,640
2	61	$123,649	$125,280
3	62	$132,305	$133,920
4	63	$141,566	$142,560
5	**64**	**$151,476**	**$151,200**
6	65	$162,079	$159,840
7	66	$173,424	$168,480
8	67	$185,564	$177,120
9	68	$198,554	$185,760
10	69	$212,452	$194,400

Do be careful to read the fine print. Some of the simple interest/higher rate-of-return products have a not-so-favorable payment schedule. Remember, there are two important factors when choosing the right FIA with a GIB rider: 1) The guaranteed rate of return (and how long the guarantee lasts) and 2) the income percentage.

HELPFUL QUESTIONS AND ANSWERS

Question—If you choose to surrender a FIA with a GIB rider, can you walk away with the guaranteed account value?

Answer—No. If you surrender the FIA, you will receive the actual account value that grows at market rates (whatever that happens to be minus fees and surrender charges).

Question—When can you activate the GIB rider to start paying you a lifetime income stream you can never outlive?

Answer—With most products, you can activate the income benefit 12 months after purchase.

Question—Can you receive more money from the guaranteed income benefit if the FIA increases in value during the payout phase?

Answer—Yes. While it's not too likely, if there is a period of very positive years in the measuring stock index, the guaranteed income benefit could increase (see the next section on a unique increasing income GIB rider where the income will definitely increase over time).

Question—Do you have to "annuitize" the FIA in order to receive the guaranteed income benefit?

Answer—No. If you want to take distributions from the FIA, you still have access to the account value (although taking withdrawals will lower the guaranteed income benefit going forward).

Question—What is the extra cost for the GIB "rider"?

Answer—It depends on the company, but the going rate seems to be between .4% (.004) and .85% (.0085) of the actual account value. This fee is taken out every year.

Question—Do GIB riders make sense with a FIA that already guarantees you will never lose money when the market goes down and where most FIAs lock in investment returns on an annual basis?

Answer—This is a tough one. Many people who are frugal or cheap will not like the idea of paying the GIB rider fee. IF the S&P 500 index has "average" returns AND you die within a few years of when you are supposed to from an actuarial standpoint, then the rider is not needed (from a pure mathematical point of view).

The rub is the "IF" and the "AND." Because we don't know when we are going to die, it's very difficult for me to not recommend the GIB rider for most people. I'm much more concerned about someone running out of money at age 85-88+ when a change in quality of life could mean the end of life than I am in the fact that a few dollars in extra fees were paid every year to have the rider (especially since the rider fee is typically ⅓ to ½ of what the typical annual mutual fund expense is).

RECEIVE AN **INCREASING INCOME** PAYMENT FROM YOUR GIB RIDER

I have one simple question to ask you: Are you interested in the **maximum amount of income** over time from your GIB rider, or are you equally concerned about what will pass (the account value of your FIA) to your heirs at death.

If your main concern or goal is to receive the **maximum amount of income** over time from your FIA GIB rider, then there is a unique product design in the market that should accomplish this goal.

The following information will not only explain how this unique GIB rider works, but the illustrations will be more "real world" because I'll be using a variable return in the FIA vs. a static level annual rate of return.

Payment options

So far I have only explained a guaranteed income for life benefit in terms of a **level payment**. An explanation of a level income benefit would be as follows—The income benefit will pay an annuity owner per the following schedule (level payment): 60-69 = 5%, 70-79 = 6%, 80-89 = 7%, 90+ = 8%.

As I previously discussed, the level options vary per company and per product.

There is an annual reset with a level income rider; but like most income riders in the industry, it's realistically only going to increase the income if the returns on the actual account value 1-2-3 years following the rider being activated are higher than the guaranteed rate of return. For this reason, the income benefit for this rider is considered a "**level**" income benefit.

Increasing income—As will be explained, a handful of products in the marketplace have what is known as an increasing income rider.

The unique part of this rider is that the **income can increase in any year there is a positive return** on the actual account value in the FIA.

For example, if the S&P 500 index as calculated in the account value of the product returned 5%, the **income benefit would be increased by 5%**.

Once the income has been increased due to a positive return on the actual account value, the new higher income payment will **never go backwards** and will **continue to increase** every year the actual account value increases.

NO FREE LUNCH

Remember, there is only so much money to go around in a FIA product that also has a GIB rider.

Logically speaking, if the FIA GIB is designed to increase the income every year the actual account value increases, the company has to have the product financially designed to still make a profit.

This unique increasing income design has three features to it that should allow the insurance company to still make a profit on the product:

1) The guaranteed accumulation account is only guaranteed to grow at 4% (vs. 6-8% like most of the other products in the marketplace).

Let me add to the definition of the guarantee. The insurance company will guarantee the annuity owner **4% every year** OR whatever the actual **account value is credited each year** (whichever is higher).

Therefore, if the actual account value is credited with 10% during the accumulation period, 10% would be credited to the guaranteed accumulation account value, not 4%.

The 4% guaranteed product has an annual reset with the guarantee and, therefore, is designed to credit any higher crediting amount to the guaranteed account every single year.

Most other products in the market will not credit a higher amount to the guaranteed account unless over a period of years (usually 5) the returns in the actual account exceed the guaranteed return (which is not likely to happen).

2) The income stream is based on the least beneficial payment schedule in the market. I explained earlier that one product in the market ratchets up income payments by one tenth of a percent every year and is calculated by taking the annuitant's age and subtracting 10.

Therefore, if an annuitant is 69 years old, with the annual ratchet GIB rider, the income benefit would be **5.9%**

With the increasing income product discussed in this section of the book, the income benefit for a 69 year old would be based on a 5% rate (from ages 60-69 the income benefit is 5%).

With the product designed to hedge some of the risk, it is priced so that the companies offering this unique and powerful rider should be able to continue to make a profit selling it.

Also keep in mind that, when the insurance company pays you more with an increasing income rider, it's simply accelerating the amount of money being removed from your actual account value.

As you will see in an upcoming example, the amount of money that will pass to the heirs when you die may be slightly or even significantly less than with an increasing income rider (which makes sense since the insurance company is paying you back more of your own money sooner).

LET'S LOOK AT THE NUMBERS

Trying to learn what an increasing income rider is and how it works from written material is difficult. However, I feel confident that when you go over the following examples you will fully understand this unique rider and why it may be just the one for you if your goal is to generate the maximum amount of guaranteed income over your lifetime.

The guaranteed accumulation account

The first issue that needs to be understood is how the 4% guaranteed return differs from the classic level guarantee.

What you need to remember is that the guarantee is the highest of 4% or whatever the return is on the actual account value every year.

The column on the right in the following chart is the amount credited to the <u>actual</u> account value every year. You'll see three years out of ten when the <u>actual</u> account value is credited with 0%. That means the S&P 500 index as calculated for the <u>actual</u> account value returned 0% on the nose or what would be more likely is that each of the three 0% years represent years when the S&P 500 had a negative rate of return (because FIAs do not partake in the downside of the market, the crediting rate in down years is 0%).

The second-to-right-hand column is the <u>actual</u> account balance.

The column in the middle that says "Return with 4% in zero years" is what is being credited to the <u>guaranteed</u> account value. In years when the return on the <u>actual</u> account is less than 4%, the return in the <u>guaranteed</u> account defaults to the minimum which is 4%.

The third column from the left is the <u>guaranteed</u> account value as it is credited with this unique crediting method.

This example is for a 60 year old who funded the FIA in year one with $500,000 in a product that has a 5% premium bonus.

Year	Age	Year End Balance	Return w/4% in zero years	Year End Balance	Hypothetical Return
1	60	$546,000	**4%**	$522,900	**0%**
2	61	$595,140	9%	$567,681	9%
3	62	$642,751	8%	$610,643	8%
4	63	$668,461	**4%**	$608,201	**0%**
5	64	$715,254	7%	$648,172	7%
6	65	$772,474	8%	$697,225	8%
7	66	$818,822	6%	$736,103	6%
8	67	$851,575	**4%**	$733,158	**0%**
9	68	$928,217	9%	$795,946	9%
10	69	**$1,002,474**	8%	**$856,183**	8%
			6.7% average		**5.5% average**

One interesting thing to note about the <u>actual</u> account value is that, in years when the return is 0%, the account value goes down. That's because with this product, when you add the guaranteed return/income for life rider, there is a .04% fee that is charged every year.

What you'll notice from the above chart is that the <u>guaranteed</u> account after 10 years has an average rate of return of 6.7%. That is less than the guarantee that most other companies offer with level income payment riders (you can find 7-8% with several companies).

The <u>actual</u> account value grew at what I would call a fairly average real-world return (5.5% over 10 years).

The conclusion from this example is that it is likely that, if you purchased a FIA with an increasing income rider, you probably would end up with a higher guaranteed accumulation value than with several other level income rider products in the marketplace.

Is that a reason NOT to buy an increasing income rider FIA? I have not given you enough information to make that decision yet.

GUARANTEED INCOME FOR LIFE

I will now discuss what happens and how this product works when you choose to activate the increasing guaranteed income for life rider (which can be activated 12 months after purchasing the annuity).

When you get into the **income phase**, this is the only product that has an **increasing income option** with the possibility to increase the income annually. Again, most products in the marketplace have a level-income option.

Starting income—When you decide to activate the guaranteed income rider, it is based on the value in your "accumulation" account (just like level-income products).

In my previous example, the accumulation account value at age 70 was **$1,002,474** (the actual account value was **$856,183**). Then depending on your age, the company will start your income stream using a certain income percentage. For the product I am illustrating, the starting income stream schedule looks as follows: 5% from ages 60-70, 5.5% from ages 70-79, and 6% from ages 80-90.

Therefore, if the example client activated the income stream at age 70 (year 11 of the contract), the income would start out at $1,002,474 x 5.5% = **$55,136**.

Again, the unique part of this rider is that the **income can increase in any year there is a positive return** in the annuity. For example, if the S&P 500 index as calculated in this product returned 8%, the income benefit would be increased by 8%.

Using the example, the income for year two would be the same as year one because the actual return in year one in the annuity equaled 0%.

In year two, however, the actual return in the product was 9%. Therefore, the income for the third year payment would increase as follows: $55,136 x 9% = $4,962 (creating a new income of = **$60,098**).

Let me illustrate the power of a guaranteed increasing income rider by extrapolating out my example until age 90. I will take the 10-year hypothetical returns from earlier (0%, 9%, 8%, 0%, 7%, 8%, 6%, 0%, 9%, 8%) and roll them for the second 10-year window. Therefore, in year 11, the return will be zero; in year 12, the return will be 9% and so on.

Age	Guaranteed Income	Actual Index Rate of Return	Age	Guaranteed Income
70	$55,136	0%	80	$93,594
71	$55,136	9%	81	$93,594
72	$60,098	8%	82	$102,018
73	$64,906	0%	83	$110,179
74	$64,906	7%	84	$110,179
75	$69,450	8%	85	$117,892
76	$75,006	6%	86	$127,323
77	$79,506	0%	87	$134,963
78	$79,506	9%	88	$134,963
79	$86,661	8%	89	$147,109

The guaranteed income numbers you'll see in the following chart will truly be stunning. Do remember that this is an example and based on the actual returns in your annuity. The income payments could be higher or lower depending on those returns.

-The total income from the first 10 years = **$690,311**.

-The total income from the second 10 years = **$1,171,814**.

-The total income for the 20-year period = **$1,862,125**.

The payments keep going even after your account value goes to zero

The question I've asked and answered a few times in this chapter is how can an insurance company afford to offer this product? Remember, the main reason is because the insurance company is giving you back your own money when making the guaranteed income payments.

In the above example, the **$55,136** payment from year one is taken out of your **actual account value**. If in the annuity the actual returns in the early years are equal to or greater than the income payment percentage, then the actual account value will not decrease or will slowly decrease. I will illustrate how this works using the numbers from my example (see the chart).

In the following chart, the second column on the left is the beginning **actual** account balance for the year, and the column on the far right is the year-end **actual** account value.

Remember, the actual account is what can be taken out of the annuity through withdrawals (in year 11 of the annuity there would be no surrender charge).

I've put into the chart the guaranteed income payment using my 10-year rolling hypothetical return. You will also see the actual returns in the annuity based on those hypothetical returns (the actual account value is still growing even though income payments are being made).

What you'll notice is that the actual account value goes to zero prior to the example client turning age 86. If the client dies prior to age 86, his/her heirs will receive the account value in the right-hand column (which is dramatically different than single-premium annuity products that typically would pass less or significantly less to the heirs upon an annuitant's death).

The main reason people buy this product is so they will know that if they live a long life they will NEVER run out of income. It's very comforting; and as you should surmise from the numbers, the income payments are very strong.

Age	Beginning Acct. Balance	Guaranteed Income Payment	Actual Returns	Ending Actual Acct. Balance
70	$856,183	$55,136	$0	$797,843
71	$797,843	$55,136	$66,844	$806,312
72	$806,312	$60,098	$59,697	$802,687
73	$802,687	$64,906	$0	$734,830
74	$734,830	$64,906	$46,895	$713,951
75	$713,951	$69,450	$51,560	$693,277
76	$693,277	$75,006	$37,096	$652,746
77	$652,746	$79,506	$0	$570,948
78	$570,948	$79,506	$44,230	$533,529
79	$533,529	$86,661	$35,749	$480,686
80	$480,686	$93,594	$0	$385,543
81	$385,543	$93,594	$26,275	$316,951
82	$316,951	$102,018	$17,195	$231,200
83	$231,200	$110,179	$0	$120,536
84	$120,536	$110,179	$725	$11,038
85	$11,038	$117,892	$0	$0
86	$0	$127,323	$0	$0
87	$0	$134,963	$0	$0
88	$0	$134,963	$0	$0
89	$0	$147,109	$0	$0

If the example client lives past 89, the income payments will continue to be paid (and will increase in any year the index return is positive in the product). I chose to stop the chart at age 89 simply for brevity purposes.

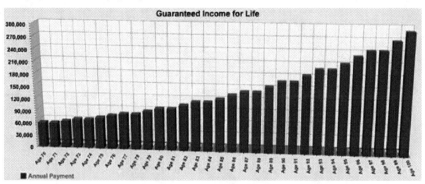

200

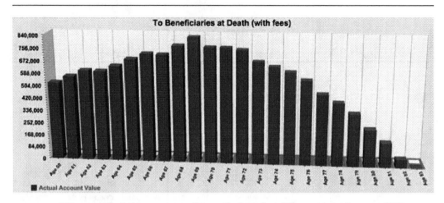

The previous two charts simply illustrate in a different manner the increasing income (first chart) and the amount of money that will pass to the heirs upon death (second chart).

COMPARING AN INCREASING INCOME RIDER TO A TYPICAL LEVEL RETURN/INCOME RIDER

I think the best way to help determine if an increasing income rider FIA can be a viable tool is to compare it to one of the better level return/level income products.

Comparison 1:

The following comparison will be what I consider to be fairly real world.

I'd like you to keep two key points in mind when looking at this comparison:

1) I assumed what I think is a reasonable rate of return over the 10 accumulation years (prior to starting the income for life payment) for the above example (a 5.5% average annual rate of return).

2) I used the same ten-year rolling return in the income phase for both products (which is driving the increased payment in positive years for the increasing income product): 0%, 9%, 8%, 0%, 7%, 8%, 6%, 0%, 9%, and 8%.

Age	GIB Increasing Income	GIB Level income
70	**$55,136**	$61,965
71	**$55,136**	$61,965
72	**$60,098**	$61,965
73	**$64,906**	$61,965
74	**$64,906**	$61,965
75	**$69,450**	$61,965
76	**$75,006**	$61,965
77	**$79,506**	$61,965
78	**$79,506**	$61,965
79	**$86,661**	$61,965
80	**$93,594**	$61,965
81	**$93,594**	$61,965
82	**$102,018**	$61,965
83	**$110,179**	$61,965
84	**$110,179**	$61,965
85	**$117,892**	$61,965
86	**$127,323**	$61,965
87	**$134,963**	$61,965
88	**$134,963**	$61,965
89	**$147,109**	$61,965
Total Income	**$1,862,125**	**$1,239,300**

The difference in income over time is staggering. The increasing income product generated **$622,825** more income than the level income product.

In the previous example, there was no comparison between how much income would be received with the level income and increasing income product. The increasing income product produced significantly more income.

Using the previous example, you need to also keep in mind that the <u>actual account value</u> that will pass to the annuity owner's beneficiaries at death will be decreased on an increasing basis as the income payments increase.

With the <u>increasing</u> income product, the actual account value went to **zero** in this example when the annuitant turned age 85.

With the <u>level</u> income product, the actual account value went to **zero** when the annuitant turned age 90.

Therefore, as I indicated earlier, the increasing income product is designed for maximum income and will most likely pass less or much less money to your heirs upon death.

Comparison 2:

What if the returns in the <u>actual</u> account value in an increasing and level income FIA are lower than what I've assumed in the previous comparison?

As you will see, lower returns significantly hurt the increasing income product. Because the guaranteed return inside the accumulation account is 4% or whatever the measuring stock index returns (if higher), the beginning balance used to determine the starting point for the guaranteed income payments will be lower for the increasing income product. Let's see how this, along with a lower average rate of return over the payout phase, affects the income stream.

I will use the following returns for the 10-year roll up period from the example client's age 60-69: 0%, 6%, 5%, 0%, 5%, 6%, 3%, 0%, 5%, and 0%. The average over the 10-year period is **3%**. I will roll the same hypothetical return starting again for ages 70-79, and 80-89.

Let's look at the numbers. I think you'll find the difference very interesting. In the following chart, I have listed the income from the previous **5.5%** average return example, the new **3%** return assumption, and the level income payment.

The level income payments are the same regardless of the actual returns (remember, income from the 7% guaranteed return with level income product typically will not vary over time).

Age	GIB Inc. Income 5.5% ave. return	GIB Inc. Income 3% ave. return	GIB Level income
70	$55,136	$45,695	$61,965
71	$55,136	$45,695	$61,965
72	$60,098	$48,437	$61,965
73	$64,906	$50,858	$61,965
74	$64,906	$50,858	$61,965
75	$69,450	$53,401	$61,965
76	$75,006	$56,606	$61,965
77	$79,506	$58,304	$61,965
78	$79,506	$58,304	$61,965
79	$86,661	$61,219	$61,965
80	$93,594	$61,219	$61,965
81	$93,594	$61,219	$61,965
82	$102,018	$64,892	$61,965
83	$110,179	$68,137	$61,965
84	$110,179	$68,137	$61,965
85	$117,892	$71,543	$61,965
86	$127,323	$75,836	$61,965
87	$134,963	$78,111	$61,965
88	$134,963	$78,111	$61,965
89	$147,109	$82,017	$61,965
Total Income	$1,862,125	$1,238,599	$1,239,300

What will jump out at you is the fact that, even with the increasing income product only returning 3% in the <u>actual account</u> value (which is very conservative), the total income from the increasing income rider is still virtually identical to the level income product ($1,238,599 vs. $1,239,300).

Comparison 3:

This is the comparison that will probably intrigue most readers. This is the "what if" comparison if the measuring stock index does very well over the years of the example.

For this last comparison, I'll assume an average rate of return of 7% in the FIA. While 5%-6% annual is realistic, in a good market run, a FIA could average 7% (especially a monthly cap product). The 10-year rolling return will be as follows (both during the accumulation period and the income period): 10%, 5%, 12%, 0%, 8%, 12%, 8%, 0%, 10%, and 5%.

Age	Inc. Income 5.5% ave. return	Inc. Income 3% ave. return	Inc. Income 7% ave. return	GIB Level income
70	$55,136	$45,695	$60,959	$61,965
71	$55,136	$45,695	$67,055	$61,965
72	$60,098	$48,437	$70,407	$61,965
73	$64,906	$50,858	$78,856	$61,965
74	$64,906	$50,858	$78,856	$61,965
75	$69,450	$53,401	$85,165	$61,965
76	$75,006	$56,606	$95,385	$61,965
77	$79,506	$58,304	$103,015	$61,965
78	$79,506	$58,304	$103,015	$61,965
79	$86,661	$61,219	$113,317	$61,965
80	$93,594	$61,219	$118,983	$61,965
81	$93,594	$61,219	$130,881	$61,965
82	$102,018	$64,892	$137,425	$61,965
83	$110,179	$68,137	$153,916	$61,965
84	$110,179	$68,137	$153,916	$61,965
85	$117,892	$71,543	$166,229	$61,965
86	$127,323	$75,836	$186,177	$61,965
87	$134,963	$78,111	$201,071	$61,965
88	$134,963	$78,111	$201,071	$61,965
89	$147,109	$82,017	$221,178	$61,965
Total Income	$1,862,125	$1,238,599	$2,526,877	$1,239,300

Using what I would consider the high end of what the potential returns could be in the increasing income FIA product, look at the difference in income as compared to the level income product: **$1,287,577** ($2,526,877 vs. $1,239,300).

SUMMARY AND CONCLUSIONS FROM THE COMPARISON EXAMPLES

If you literally want a "guaranteed income for life," you should buy a FIA with a level return/level income rider.

With a level return/level income product you know exactly what your income benefit will be when you activate the rider. In my previous comparisons, that amount is $61,965.

While that income amount could increase if the measuring index has a really good run over a period of years, the vast majority of the time, your income once started will remain level until you die.

If you want a product that over time should pay you either more income with what I would call average returns in the measuring stock index over time, you should buy an increasing income rider FIA.

The caveats to the above statements are as follows:

1) If your goal is a guaranteed income but also that of passing wealth to your heirs through the actual account value at your death, then an increasing income product may not be the one. Because the increasing income payments can be significantly more over time than a level income payment, your actual account value with the increasing income product may go to zero much quicker than a level income product.

2) If you plan on waiting more than 10 years before activating the income rider, you may not want to use an increasing income product because the maximum guarantee roll up rate is ten years. If you want to wait until 12-15+ years before activating income, using a level income product that allows for a guaranteed roll up rate over a longer time span may work out better for you.

3) If you plan on funding a FIA with a guaranteed income rider and activating the income 12 months after funding or even within a few years of funding, the numbers strongly indicate that using an increasing income FIA will provide you significantly more income over your life expectancy.

SUMMARY ON GUARANTEED INCOME BENEFIT RIDERS ON FIXED INDEXED ANNUITIES

If your head is spinning with all the numbers I've thrown at you in this chapter, don't worry. The bottom line with GIB riders on FIAs is very simple to understand.

The benefits to a FIA with a GIB rider are as follows:

1) Your money will **never go backwards** when the stock market declines.

2) You will be given a **guaranteed rate of return** of between 4-8% on an accumulation account inside the product.

3) You will be given a **guaranteed income for life** you can never outlive (which is based on the guaranteed accumulation account value when activated).

The income stream at a minimum with most level income products will be paid based on the following rates of return:

5% at ages 60-69
6% at ages 70-79
7% at ages 80-89
8% at ages 90+

4) You have **access to the money** in your FIA at all times (subject to the typical surrender charges).

5) When you die, the account value will **pass to your beneficiaries**.

6) The guaranteed rate of return can **roll up for 15+ years** with certain products.

7) With some products, your guaranteed income for life can **increase by 3%** if you can't perform 2 of your 6 ADLs (a free quasi long-term care benefit).

It's really that simple. If you like the bullet points above, you are a candidate to grow your wealth with a FIA that has a GIB benefit rider.

Maximum income

If you would like to buy a product that has a good likelihood to pay you the maximum amount of income, you should purchase an increasing income rider product.

Fees

The fees for GIB riders typically range from .4% a year to .85% a year (which is significantly less than a typical mutual fund).

YOU ARE NOT A CANDIDATE TO USE A GIB RIDER

If you answer yes to the following questions, you are not a candidate to grow wealth with a GIB rider:

1) You do not mind risking all of your money in the stock market (and subjecting it to 59% downturns/crashes as we've seen during 2007-2009).

2) You are not interested in guaranteeing that you will have a specific annual income every year in retirement that you can never outlive.

3) You have more than 15 years to wait before needing income from your retirement funds.

QUESTIONS

While I hope I've done a good job with my explanation of how GIB riders work within the context of a FIA, I'm sure that many readers will have questions.

If you have questions, please feel free to e-mail me at roccy@retiringwithoutrisk.com; or you can also go to www.retiringwithoutrisk.com and submit a question through the web-site.

Remember, at www.retiringwithoutrisk.com, you can also get temporary access to my proprietary GIB rider calculator so you can determine how much guaranteed income for life your current wealth can generate for you.

Help from the Author

I hesitated when determining whether to have a section in the book titled, "Help from the Author."

Why?

Because I do not take on individual clients anymore.

What I do for a living is educate advisors on the proper way to give the best advice to their clients.

I still put together comprehensive memos for clients telling them what they need to do to become asset protected, get their estate plans in order, reduce income, estate and capital gains taxes and, of course, how to position themselves to Retire Without Risk.

However, these clients are not mine but those of the advisors I work with.

Even so, when you put out an educational book for the general public like this book, I believe you have a duty to readers to answers questions they may have after reading the book.

Therefore, I have created a web-site for readers to go to so they can receive more information than what I was able to put in this book and be able to submit questions to me.

The web-site is **www.retiringwithoutrisk.com**.

On that site, you can **submit a question** that will go directly to my e-mail inbox. Unless I'm traveling, I typically answer e-mails nearly ten hours a day; and so if you submit a question, you can be assured to have it answered in very short order.

Also, on the site, you can find the **33-page white paper** I alluded to in the book where I compare guaranteed income riders (GIBs) on both Variable Annuities (VAs) and the Fixed Indexed Annuities (FIAs) you read about in this book.

As I stated, VAs have been offering GIB riders for years and FIAs are the new kid on the block. Because most securities licensed advisors (who drive the majority of financial/retirement planning advice in this country) know very little, if anything, about

FIAs, I felt it was important for advisors and non-advisors reading this book to be able to compare the riders of both products.

The white paper in some respects does a more complete job of explaining GIB riders (albeit in a bit more technical fashion).

VIEW MULTIPLE VOICED-OVER POWERPOINT PRESENTATIONS

Also on the web-site you can view multiple voiced-over educational PowerPoint presentations such as:

1) FIAs (basic learning presentation)

2) GIB riders (how they work)

3) Increasing income GIB riders (how they work and why they can provide significantly more income than level income riders)

4) Tax-free retirement (how to grow wealth in a tax-free manner using Revolutionary Life).

There are other presentations on the web-site as well, such as basic estate planning, asset protection, charitable planning, etc. I figured if readers were going to go to the site to learn more about the topics covered in this book, many would also be interested in other topics that affect their wealth.

WHAT IF YOU WANT HELP PICKING A PRODUCT DISCUSSED IN THIS BOOK?

The answer depends. You can send me an e-mail or submit a form on the web-site asking me a question; and if you provide me with enough information, I'll give you my opinion.

However, I know that many readers will want to talk with a local advisor and sit down to talk with one face to face.

Over time, I've educated hundreds of advisors from all over the country. The chances that I have someone in your local area who can help you are significant.

As you found out when reading this book, while the general concepts/products discussed in this book are not the most difficult in the world, when you really get down to how to design and pick products that are best for an individual's situation, it is really important to work with an advisor who knows what he/she is doing.

As I stated in the beginning of this book, if an advisor gave you this book for you to read and to learn from, the chances are significant that the advisor understands what I discussed and should be able to counsel you appropriately. I can't personally vouch for them; but just by the way this book has been written, an advisor who hands it out better know what's in the book and be able to give advice to a client accordingly.

If an advisor did not give you this book and you'd like to find one who can help you, please feel free to e-mail me at **roccy@retiringwithoutrisk.com;** and I'd be happy to refer you to someone in your local area. Or you can also go to **www.retiringwithoutrisk.com** and submit a form that will come directly to me.

Whether you e-mail me or submit the form online, please give me as much information as you feel comfortable with so I can refer you to the advisor who can best help you. It is likely that I have multiple advisors in your local area; and based on your individual situation, one advisor vs. another may be better for you to work with.

SECOND GUSSING SOMEONE ELSE'S ADVICE

While advisors may not care for it, one of the things that gives me the most enjoyment in my professional life is pointing out to someone why the advisor they have been working with may not be giving advice I think is "client friendly."

My guess is that many people who read this book will be somewhat upset at the advice they've been given over the years. If you had all of your money in the stock market and saw it crash with the stock market between 2007-2009, I'm sure you are not happy.

If you wonder if the advice you've been given in the past or are being given from an advisor who is trying to pick up your business, you should feel free to e-mail me or fill out a form for submission on my web-site; and I'd be happy to give you my opinion (or refer you to a local advisor who knows what he/she is doing and can give you an opinion).

If you are simply looking for affirmation that the advice you've been given is good advice, I will provide that affirmation if that's my opinion after reviewing your situation.

BOOK REVIEW

If you are so motivated in a good or bad way from reading this book, I would appreciate your feedback. Positive feedback confirms that the way I write books is understandable and helpful to readers.

If you want to provide constructive criticism (or complain) about something in the book or the way I wrote something, please feel free to submit such comments. That will help me when I update the book (which I will do on an annual basis); and since it is my goal to put forth the best book I can, negative or constructive comments are welcome.

Thank you for buying this book, and please do not hesitate to go to www.retiringwithoutrisk.com for more information and to get answers to your questions.

C